ARCHITECTURAL
GUIDES FOR TRAVELERS

·

ISLAMIC SPAIN

GODFREY GOODWIN

CHRONICLE BOOKS · SAN FRANCISCO

First published in the United States in 1990 by Chronicle Books.

Series conceived by Georgina Harding
Editor: Gabrielle Townsend
Series design: Clare Finlaison
Design: Wendy Bann
Maps and plans: David Woodroffe
Picture research: Emma Milne
Index: Hilary Bird

Printed in The Netherlands by Giethoorn, Meppel

Library of Congress Cataloging-in-Publication Data:
Goodwin, Godfrey
    Islamic Spain / Godfrey Goodwin
      p.   cm. — (Architectural guides for travelers)
    Includes bibliographical references.
    ISBN 0-87701-692-5
    1. Architecture. Islamic—Spain—Guide-books.   2.
    Architecture—Spain—Guide-books.   3. Spain—Civilization.
    Islamic—Guide-books.
    I. Title II. Series.
NA1303.G6   1990
720'.8'82971—dc20   89-24029
                                                          CIP

10 9 8 7 6 5 4 3 2 1

Chronicle Books
275 Fifth Street
San Francisco, California 94103

CONTENTS

PREFACE

There are three good reasons for visiting Islamic Spain. The great monuments, such as the Alhambra at Granada or the mosque at Córdoba, are world-famous but there are other fine buildings which are less familiar. There are gaunt but romantic fortresses and towers. There is also the all-pervading memory of this period of Spain's history, and not only in Andalucía. It lingers in the vocabulary of farming life and in the light and shade of crofts and narrow lanes of villages in the hills.

There are other intangible reasons. It was from Toledo that much of the learning of Hellenic times was transmitted to Europe after the Christian reconquest following exploration of the Muslim libraries. On the other hand there are tracts of country from Extremadura to Castile where the region of war, blackened by the battles of invasion and reconquest, still bears scars.

This book attempts to reveal the outstanding remains of the Islamic contribution to Spain and its culture. It draws attention to the cross-fertilization which was so important to the marriage of Western and Eastern ideas. Although it is wise to bear in mind how intolerant all religions and sects were during the great span of years from 712 to 1492 (a period as long as that from King John to the building of the Channel Tunnel), it is also important to remember how often both princes and common folk ignored religious obsessions and married husbands and wives from opposing faiths for love or profit or from simple political expediency.

The book is organized by centres such as Sevilla, Córdoba and Granada, except where Islamic traces are so slight that no one city can serve as a focus, in which case sites are listed within the relevant province. This is particularly true of Spain north of the River Tagus. Each centre is studied in a sequence of major and minor monuments and then follows an alphabetical list of surrounding towns, villages and sites. No attempt is made to cover every fortress or watch tower, many of which are still unstudied and have origins which are disputed by the leading scholars.

(*Opposite*) Granada, the Alhambra: the Sala de los Reyes, adjoining the Patio de los Leones.

FRANCE

Llançà

NAVARRA

Tudela Huesca CATALUÑA Girona

Tarazona Tauste ARAGÓN Balaguer
Ágreda Borja
Añón Utebo
Rueda de Jalón Zaragoza Lerida Terrassa
Tobed
Calatayud Longares
Cariñena
Ateca Paniza
Torrigo
Maluenda Burbaguena
Daroca Tortosa
Calamocha
Molina de Aragón San Martin del Río

Albarracín
Teruel Benasal

Alcalá de Chisvert

N

ANCHA Cardenete Sagunto

Alarcón Buñol Valencia
VALENCIA Cullera
Albacete Játiva

Jumilla Alicante

Monteagudo
MURCIA Murcia

ALUCÍA Cartagena

Baza
Guadix
Mojácar
Berja Almería

CHRISTIAN
SPAIN
León

Zaragoza

Madrid
Toledo
ISLAMIC SPAIN – Valencia
AL ANDALUS
Alicante
Córdoba Jaén Murcia
Sevilla Granada
Cádiz Almería
Málaga
Gibraltar

Spain in the early eighth century

QUE
NCES
olla
A RIOJA
oria
erlanga
e Duero
ma de Aragón
dinaceli
ienza
alajara

ix

Travelling in Spain

The state of the highways is improving and new motorways (relatively uncrowded because a toll is payable) are opening, although the leisured traveller would often do better to take the older roads and not avoid the villages on the way. Conditions vary according to the seasons but all roads are usually passable except in the mountains during the bitterest weeks of winter. In some areas there are roads which should only be taken after seeking local advice for one reason or another and this includes those crossing wildlife reserves.

The Government and local tourist offices issue leaflets giving the opening times of museums and monuments but there can be disappointments. Medinat az-Zahra' is a particular example, appearing to open and close at whim. Visitors should remember that everything, from shops to palaces, normally closes from 1 or 2 p.m. till 4 or 5 p.m. Many churches are only open when there is a service but can usually be visited early in the morning or at the time of evening mass.

Some fortresses are lonely places even when situated immediately above a town and sensible precautions should be taken against robbery.

INTRODUCTION

Before it was invaded by Roman legions in the second and third centuries BC, Spain was inhabited by the Iberians who left behind superb cave paintings such as those of Altamira. (The term 'Iberian' should be understood in the same spirit as that of 'Ancient Britons'. They are those eternal people who endure the arrival of invaders, marry and absorb them and themselves slowly change. Anthropologists may play a guessing game recognizing their descendants all over the Peninsula.)

The coming of the Romans literally opened up the country and, as elsewhere, their roads and bridges underlie the communications system in Spain to this day. The country prospered and towns grew under the rule of law; minorities such as Jews flourished and built up a trade across Europe and Asia. Roman-cut stone or ashlar was to be used and re-used by each successive culture which followed in the wake of the fallen empire. Byzantine rule was no longer respected after the reign of Justinian and the adventuring Visigoths overran rather than conquered the country. They relied on local bishops and senior clergy who were the only educated defence against total barbarism. Apollonius, Archbishop of Clermont, whom they much liked, described these previously nomadic warriors from east of Europe in a poem translated by Helen Waddell:

> They will not come to you at dawn
> Breathing out leeks and ardour,
> Big cheerful souls with appetites
> Much greater than my larder.

The Visigoths were countrymen who felt ill-at-ease in cities but they were converted from the Arian heresy, that Christ was less than God, to Roman Catholicism. Their ignorance of trade ruined the Jewish merchants and consequently the towns were ruined also. This meant that the peasants had to be sternly taxed and were as hostile to their masters as were the burghers. There was no money with which to pay an army and a feudal system was not established either. The

1

Visigoths lacked either natural or legal rules of succession and their last leader, Roderick or **Rodrigo**, was elected king with difficulty and his authority was not acknowledged everywhere in Spain. So it was that by AD 710 Spain was a wasted land unfit to defend itself.

The legend goes that Rodrigo carried off the beautiful daughter of the Exarch or Governor of Ceuta, the Christian Julian, who was a vassal of the Muslim ruler in Damascus, al-Walid. This **Umayyad** prince, descendant of Umar, the henchman of the Prophet Muhammad, was the recognized successor of the founder of the Islamic religion and held the paramount title of Caliph, with all the temporal authority of the Prophet but not his spiritual omnipotence.

The Caliph advised **Musa**, his commander in the Maghrib — the western region of North Africa — to reconnoitre Spain. Musa was cautious and devolved the command on his lieutenant, **Tariq**. Tariq's existence is disputed but, even if he is a myth, nevertheless somebody must have been in command. In July 710 the intrepid lieutenant crossed the Straits in the Exarch's boats with 400 cavalry and 400 foot. But after he had landed at Tarifa, 5,000 more men rallied to his standard; his, because history in the eighth century favoured outstanding personalities, especially those endowed with good fortune. Rodrigo had established his base at Algeciras which Tariq's horsemen raided until the Visigoths were lured out of their encampment and routed. No trace was found of the king, and such followers as escaped were caught up with at Écija and finally defeated.

There was nobody to stop Tariq now. He took Toledo, then the greatest city in Spain, without a fight. Only in Córdoba was he frustrated. A group of knights resisted courageously for many months. In July 712, Musa landed in Spain with 7,000 men and met up with Tariq at Talavera on the Tagus. From there he took the road to Narbonne and crossed the Pyrenees.

Almost all Spain, but not quite all, was now al-Andalus. (This was the Arabic name for Islamic Spain, not to be confused with the province of Andalucía.) Al-Andalus stretched across France as far as the Muslim tents were pitched. The nominal provincial capital of Qayrawan (Kairouan) in what is now Tunisia was too far away to control events. Alarmed at Tariq's and Musa's victories and growing power, the Caliph summoned both to Baghdad in March

716. But the conquests continued with the fall of Málaga and Elvira, while Murcia became a vassal state.

In 717 the capital was moved from Toledo to Córdoba, which was all too far away from the north-western garrison towns. These proved too weak to withstand the remnants of the Visigoth aristocracy once it had found a forceful leader in Alfonso I of Asturias. By fire and axe, he created the *al-ghaznas*, great swathes of waste where the blackened earth could not sustain an invading army. Meanwhile, the Muslims reached Autun in Burgundy and then marched

An Almohad banner captured by the Christians in 1212 (museum of the Convento de las Huelgas, Burgos).

along the banks of the Loire until their defeat by Charles Martel in 732 on an unknown field between Poitiers and Tours. The Muslim sally into Europe had been no more important to them than a foray. To the Christians, however, it was a victory which resounded like the slamming of the door in the faces of the invaders of an alien faith. Later the Christian reconquest was to slow down because there were too few people to occupy and hold the new territories. But the Muslim forces had not been reinforced because of a Berber revolt. (The Berbers were the original inhabitants of the Maghrib before the invasions of the Arabs. Their strongholds were in the Atlas Mountains and they were primarily shepherds, although, like nomads almost everywhere, whose wealth must be easily portable, they produced memorable jewellery.) Their presence in great numbers in the Muslim armies and their settlement of many parts of Spain was to give the erroneous name Moorish to a civilization which was much more than Berber. Their admirers could claim that their patient farming tamed the uplands of Spain; their detractors could claim that their rebelliousness was to sap the strength of Islamic culture.

The new Islamic lands were now to take form. It is significant that in the early years the courts of the rulers spoke Romance like their Mozarab subjects, the Christians who remained behind after the flight of the Visigoths and who enjoyed some legal and social autonomy, retaining the bishops and metropolitans. The Muslim judiciary, the *Ulama*, were afraid that the tenets of the faith would not be observed, since Arabic was the language of all Islam. It was, however, only after much preaching by these religious lawyers that Arabic was firmly established as the language of government. The life of the peasant farmers, artisans and trading Jews continued whatever the ruling religion and for these an Islamic peace was preferable to war.

*   *   *

On 7 July 750 the pleasure-loving house of Umar was overthrown by the **Abbasids** and a new Caliph ruled from Baghdad. The old family was massacred except for young **'Abd ar-Rahman**. His brother was cut down, hesitant on a river bank because he could not swim, but 'Abd ar-Rahman escaped with his loyal slave Badir, whom he had freed. The prince was hunted across Africa and was nearly trapped.

4

His mother had been a member of the Nafza Berber tribe and he sought refuge with his kinsmen, but they were hostile and he fled again, to be hunted to the shores of the sea. Badir had gone on ahead into Spain and 'Abd ar-Rahman found a boat and followed him. Syrian refugees from Abbasid repression had already reached Andalucía and were won over. Thus, after five years, 'Abd ar-Rahman landed at the age of 24 at Almuñécar on 24 August 755 and claimed the emirate.

Trained in adversity, the prince had the gift of winning followers. He entered Sevilla in March 756 but did not dawdle. The governor, **Yusuf**, had raised an army which 'Abd ar-Rahman defeated outside Córdoba in May. Yusuf continued to resist until 759, when he was killed near Toledo. Many dependants of the former Umayyad caliphs were unpopular with the established Arab immigrants, fractious Berbers and other discontented elements. Famine in 760 and a Berber revolt in the north-west endangered the Muslim hold on the country but with determination and persuasiveness the new ruler reigned for 33 years. He recruited a small professional army made up of slaves, many of whom came from Europe. There were Viking raids to repel as well as a Christian resurgence. The first Arab invaders included dispossessed landless men, criminals and political refugees, among whom were scholars whose beliefs threatened Qu'ranic absolutes. The army lived on booty and ransom, and old soldiers were given conquered lands to settle. The local peasantry was shackled by taxation. The Umayyad emirs sought prosperity and the splendours of a rich and intellectually stimulating court. They let anyone convert to Islam and there were relationships with the Christian kingdoms and intermarriage — Musa himself had married a princess from Navarre. By the tenth century Córdoba was one of the most splendid cities in Europe and its market the most extensive.

A weak monarch with over-ambitious vezirs brought the dynasty to an end and the loosely patched state split at the seams. A period during which more than 30 petty princedoms rivalled each other was distinguished by a few courts like Sevilla. Disunity exposed these titbits to larger mouths such as those of the Christian princes, to whom many of the **Ta'ifa Reyes**, as these princelings were called, paid substantial tribute. Their virtue was that many saw themselves

5

primarily as Spaniards; they were lax Muslims whose cohesion melted together with their fervour.

It was a time of retreat for Islamic Spain, symbolized by the capture of Toledo by Alfonso VI of Castile and the ambivalence of El Cid. But between 1063 and 1082 a confederation of Berber clans akin to the desert Tuareg, and so known as the Veiled Ones, conquered Morocco and built a capital at Marrakesh. It was a puritanical society, in which music and wine were banned. The frightened Muslim princes in Spain appealed to these **Almoravids** for help and the **Emir Yusuf** responded. His Berber army crossed into Spain, retook Badajoz and kept the forces of Castile at a wary distance. His power was paramount throughout Islamic Spain, which he united with North Africa. This Yusuf was an extraordinary character for he was 70 years old and had a voice which rasped and squeaked like the armour of Don Quixote. He is remembered for introducing the camel to Spain. His achievements soon silenced the mockery of Córdoba, and by 1102 his empire stretched from Aragón to Senegal. His son was softened by good living and lost the respect of his Berber troops when he succeeded in 1106, ruling only because he could pay for a mercenary army.

A rebellion lead by the **Almohad** Berbers resulted in the massacre of the Almoravids in Marrakesh in 1147. The former were Unitarians with an absolute belief in the singular nature of God and were even more puritanical than their predecessors. Their subjugation of Islamic Spain was brief because the Christian advance had become inevitable; their rule ended in 1184. A slow dwindling of Muslim power followed until only the **Nasrids** in Granada remained as tributaries of Castile until the final surrender came in 1492.

The expulsion of the Muslim population was never total except in Aragón, where their departure impoverished the province almost overnight. Elsewhere, people survived as disguised or true Christians and some even retained their Arabic names. It was the Jews who suffered worst, driven away to enrich Europe and the Ottoman Empire.

Religion

Islam began in the seventh century AD. Its prophet **Muhammad** received the verses of the Qu'ran both in trances and from the lips of the Archangel Gabriel. It was the Word

Sevilla, the Alcázar: detail of the Salón de los Reyes Moros showing the use of calligraphy in decoration and the ceramic dado with its interlace pattern of stars.

taken from the original Book enshrined in Heaven. There were to be emendations and disputed passages and interpolations besides the *Hadiths*, sayings transmitted from memories of conversations with the Prophet. Muhammad's magnetism and the force of the Qu'ran united the tribes of Arabia and in AD 622 he escaped the reactionary leaders in Mecca and proclaimed the Faith in Madina where he was to be buried. Arabia was aroused, and following the old trade routes into Greater Syria, overwhelmed the flaccid Byzantine provinces. Expansion went on and on over the centuries, both across Africa and into Europe as far as the Danube, as well as into Persia and North India.

Like all religions, Islam is divided. The **Sunni** orthodox school is its trunk; but this statement would be vehemently contested by the **Shi'ites** whose stronghold is Iran. The Sunnis are divided into four schools, of which the Malikite was dominant in Spain. The sect was and is the strictest of the Sunni schools and, for example, will not usually admit unbelievers into their mosques. Such was their severity that the *Ulama* or Fathers of the Faith sought to expel the laxer Hanafite adherents from Spain although the Christian threat made such divisions dangerous.

There were Berber and Yemeni revolts against this elite but they were short-lived, as sectarian movements depended on a charismatic leader who, once dead, left no ideas behind. Various *Mahdis* or fake reincarnations of the sublime Imam or Prophet were easy to put down. More sinister were the Isma'ilis from Alamut in Iran who, drugged or not, used assassination and terror to advance their cause. The Arab population had little reason to revolt but the Berbers yearned for autonomy. These mountain tribesmen looked down on the easy life of the towns. They were full of old superstitions and pagan beliefs and did little more than nod towards Islam until the coming of the Almoravids and the Almohads.

The Arab population was divided between Syrians, the people of the Maghrib, Yemenis and many others, but they did not find it difficult to abandon their own natal sectarianisms for the Malikite rule. Nor were there many dervish or Sufi sects in Spain. Sufi mysticism is adaptable and the members of a brotherhood sometimes remained in the newly captured provinces to establish religious strongholds from which to set up civil government. In times of peace these *rabats* lost their military characteristics and also their political importance. Some dervish movements were fanatical but most were mystical and allowed wine drinking; although they probably were not as lax as they were reputed to be, they could not flourish under a Malikite *Ulama*.

Christians and Jews, respected by Islam as 'People of the Book' (meaning the Old and New Testaments), had given prophets like Abraham and Jesus to early Islam and so were treated reasonably, unless local politics required scape-goats. Unlike mercenaries hired from Europe, the local Christians did not perform military service but paid a poll tax instead. But skilled hands were too few not to be valued as farm labourers and craftsmen, while medicine was largely practised by Jewish doctors.

There are few Spanish saints and martyrs for whom Islam was responsible but the Muslims could be fierce if provoked. Santa Columba of Córdoba was unwise when her convent at Tabanos was closed. She went to the magistrate to affirm that Muhammad was a false prophet and was beheaded. In 859 Leocritia abjured Islam and embraced Christianity. The girl was taken in by St Elogius who was about to be consecrated Archbishop of Toledo. 'I would have done as much for you,' he told the judge, refused to apostasize and was beheaded. Four days later Leocritia was also executed and, poetically, they were buried together in the cathedral at Oviedo.

The Cultivation of Mind and Land

Spain is a constellation of mountains and streams with shallow coastal plains watered by magnificent spring rivers that are mere wallows in summer. Valleys, whether spacious or narrow, are difficult of access, a division which affects local customs. For these reasons no invader was omnipotent and no culture could spread evenly over a land like a loaf with too much crust and too little fertile crumb.

The Muslims found the Roman irrigation schemes clogged up; they repaired some and enhanced others, while adding works of their own. They were expert at sinking wells and from Syria they brought the *noria* or lofty waterwheel. They introduced aubergines, artichokes, apricots, sugar-cane and almonds along with cumin, henna, madder and saffron. They established the mulberry tree and the silkworm. Southern Muslims cooked with oil while the less fortunate Christians used lard from the domestic pig, since in the colder north no olive tree could grow. Vines abounded and wine was drunk by most people, not only by poets. Cork forests were extended and flocks improved. The south had been culti-vated since Neolithic times but the Moreno sheep was probably the greatest Berber gift to Spain and then to Europe. In the lonely foothills and wide plains of Extremadura and elsewhere the lament of a lonely shepherd, with only his own dirges for company, was until recently a true link with Spain's Islamic past.

The *alcarraza*, the pitcher which cools by evaporation; the rebirth of the cart, forgotten since Roman times; the saddle and the saddle-bag; ice-cream made with mountain snow; the kerchief instead of the turban; the *sombrero; gazpacho* soup; the fine bread of Sevilla; superb horses: all these were left behind by the Muslims. Other customs have died out. Ladies no longer sit on cushions as Lady Fanshawe did in the 17th century when visiting the Queen of Spain. Hotels have been transformed since the mid-19th century when that first great writer in English on Spain, Richard Ford, said that they were bad because to make money out of travellers was repugnant to Muslims.

Other innovations had a lasting influence. The Muslims founded trade guilds, craftsmen – potters, weavers and workers in metal – were rewarded, and world trade flourished in the hands of the Jews. Caskets and jars were influenced by Byzantine work; metalwork in bronze and later in silver and gold is often difficult to distinguish from Islamic work elsewhere. In spite of the development of silk weaving in the tenth and eleventh centuries, brocades were imported from Syria and Constantinople. During the same period faience came from Iran and Iraq, but the kilns of Spain were to develop their own *cuerda seca* or cloisonné ware as well as that lustreware that reached an apotheosis in the Hispano-Mauresque platter.

The destruction of the libraries which followed on the reconquest deprived Islamic culture of its finest achievement in Spain, with a few exceptions such as the manuscripts in the Escorial library. Calligraphy, the means by which God transmitted truth to man, was the Muslims' greatest art. This does not mean that the depiction of the human form or face is a sin, as is sometimes asserted, except among fanatics. The miniature is Islamic art personified and the Spanish master-pieces were burnt along with the rest. That the bulk of the remaining architectural decoration made use of natural forms or of calligraphy is true: some of its voluptuous tendrils are far from austere. The little pictorial art that has survived is all the more precious because it is the last raindrop from the showers of a lost springtime.

The Islamic rulers set up an equitable tax system, imposing

a tithe on Muslims, imposts on the rents of state lands and a value-added tax, apart from customs duties on imports and goods in transit. The revenues from taxation supported a standing army and provided a life of luxury for the court, including beauties guarded by eunuchs whose presence at that time was universal, whether protecting women or singing in the Vatican choir. Emirs owned great libraries and attracted poets, philosophers, mathematicians and musicians to their courts which were true centres of civilization, concerned with more than just fine food and firework displays. A natural dignity lent itself to the cultivation of good manners, reflected in court poetry and works of art and literature. There was also popular poetry, which influenced the troubadours of Provence and hence the whole literary tradition of western Europe.

Two centuries after the reconquest of Toledo the works of

Astrolabe made in Toledo in 1068 by Ibrahim b. Sacid as-Sahli.

Avicenna, **Averroës** and **Arabi** (as they were known in Europe), among many others, were to influence thought in the West, even if Dante perforce had to lodge them in purgatory. Avicenna (Ibn Sina), d. 1037, the philosopher and physician, was a Neoplatonist who believed that everything derives from God and in that sense is eternal. Averroës (Ibn Rushd), d. 1198, was a follower of Aristotle whose commentaries on the Greek philosophers were to influence European thinkers such as St Thomas Aquinas. Ibn al-'Arabi, d. 1240, was a mystic who had seen Muhammad in a vision. He taught that all life is one being which is the Divine and that therefore all religions are one and the same; in the end, all atoms will return to the Light from our present outer darkness. **Maimonides** was a physician but was threatened as an unbeliever and escaped to Cairo. Among his many works was a treatise on how to grow cotton. **Gerard of Cremona** translated the *Almagest* (or mathematical tables of the fixed stars) but an error of one degree in the rate of precession, which had been corrected by al-Battni in 880 but escaped notice, was not adjusted until the 19th century. The black poet-minister **Ziryab** added a chord to the guitar, a chord which, according to the poets, pulses like the human heart. (He will be discussed under Córdoba.)

The Visigoths despised Roman baths but modest versions were built by the Muslims; many of these were later closed by those monks who believed dirt to be a symbol of purity, although others kept themselves scrubbed, since tomorrow could be Judgement Day.

Ladino, the tongue of Sephardic Jews, and Calo, that of the gypsies who came later to Spain, are gone or debased but many Arabic words live on. They have even travelled from Spain to Britain, often in the names of fruits and herbs. There are also abstract concepts such as 'nadir' from *nazir* and 'race' from the Spanish *raza*, itself from the Arabic *ra's*, meaning head, as well as everyday words such as 'guitar' from *guitarra* from *qitar*. A great number of agricultural terms have survived in Spanish, together with the familiar cry of *Ole! Ole!* which really does descend from Allah! Allah!

Islamic architecture in Spain

The Muslims arrived in Spain to find some Roman monuments

Sevilla: the surviving city walls.

standing or re-used by the Visigoths whose horseshoe arch had Roman and possibly Iberian antecedents. Their modest basilicas employed Roman ashlar and columns. The tradition of using brick, universal in Byzantine territories, also flourished.

The early Muslim builders were soldiers and therefore used to constructing stone defences. They took the heavier ashlar to use in the footings of walls where these could be built directly on the bare rock. The stones grew smaller as the walls grew higher because of the difficulty of hoisting large blocks; smaller stones were also more economical to use, once the ashlar frame was established. The period of **'Abd ar-Rahman II** (r. 822–852) saw the combination of headers and stretchers which created a rhythm to the stone courses, while in the reign of **al-Hakam II** (961–976) decoration combined with economy to produce oblong blocks smaller than before, like books upon a shelf. Stone was also encased in brick in the Byzantine manner, a portent of the **Mudéjar** style, which was developed by Muslim craftsmen who continued to work for Christian patrons.

The Muslims brought with them the skill to build castles which carried the mathematics of defence to an unsurpassed degree of sophistication, invincible until the use of gunpowder. In the ninth century they introduced the bent entry, a single turning at right angles to the gate which exposed the attacker in a confined space under a machicoulis, or hole in the vaulting, through which stones or worse could be dropped on the heads of a foe. This refinement had developed in Syria and spread through Muslim territories into Europe. A soldier had to be a skilled mason, for it was essential to raise walls to chin height within hours; the whole fortress might take less than three months to build.

The first Umayyad castles in Spain followed a Byzantine pattern of round towers united by stretches of curtain wall to form a square or rectangle, but by the 11th century castles conformed to the terrain and were extended to cover a ridge or escarpment. Often there was only one gate created by bringing two towers close together; a postern, as at Mérida, was rare. Once the walls of the fortress were complete, cisterns were dug in the rock because the fortress was more likely to be taken by siege than by assault. Castles served as banks for tax collectors and as police stations which controlled town or country. Some developed tunnels

Fortifications at
Niebla.

and later ones were built of concrete, a single mixture of
mortar and small stones, where cut stone was scarce. Bigger
fortresses were carefully planned and the use of ashlar in
quantity is indicative of a royal commission.

A significant development which never became popular
elsewhere in Europe was the *albarrani* tower which is seen
at its most spectacular at Talavera or at Cáceres. This was a
salient tower which outflanked the walls by as much as 8.5 m
(29 ft) and was connected by a bridge, complete with
machicoulis, of its own height. Two such arms caught the
attacker inside three walls of fire. However, it is disputed
whether such towers belong to a relatively early Islamic
period or to Mudéjar builders under Christian rule two
hundred years later.

All cities in the Middle Ages suffered from outbursts of mob
violence, in Islam called *fitna*, or an offence against the
Faith, for to challenge or murder a ruler was to challenge or
murder mercy. In Spain the term refers expressly to the years
1008–1031 when the Caliphate of Córdoba was overthrown. Because of these gangs, the rulers moved out of
their citadels into fortified country mansions. An emir might
own several estates like those which still surround Marrakesh.
The air would be fresh, the hunting good and the peasantry
unlikely to disturb their master. In the city grand town houses
sheltered behind strong doors and even the emir's apartments were restricted to one or two courtyards within fortress
walls. There was no multiplicity of rooms and the modest

offices of government officials were kept apart. Patios were graced by pools which softly lit and cooled the inner halls and reflected the arcades, while fountains splashed and glittered. The patios were the only gardens, for, as with Roman villas, and then the Umayyad desert palaces, the ground around the palaces would have been woods, orchards and market gardens; their pools were tanks needed for irrigation, fed by spring or conduit. In Iran walled gardens developed but in Spain orchards were enough. That al-Andalus was known as the Garden, in the sense that all gardens reflect the myth of Eden and Heaven, is true. But Paradise has always been depicted by humans in terms of their experience and the Islamic garden in Spain derives from Roman, not Qu'ranic, antecedents.

Very few mosques remain. The larger of them usually reflected the parent mosque of Damascus, which had previously been a church shared for a time with Christians. The same arrangement was agreed at Córdoba but goodwill ages, and at both places the Christians were eventually bought out and a proper mosque built. Thus circumstance created a hall of many columns much broader than it was long, with a central aisle wider than those flanking it, although Islam is not a processional religion. The *mihrab* niche was marked by a handsome dome. The mosque was approached through an open courtyard which in Damascus was surrounded by cool arcades, whereas the Córdoba mosque was only walled because in the centre it was planted with aisles of orange trees for shade. The architectural historian Henri Terrasse pointed out that Umayyad engineers had difficulty erecting stone or brick vaults when they needed to roof large areas, until the astonishing elaboration of those wooden jigsaws or *muqarnas* or stalactite domes which are the glory of the Alhambra. Nor was there any impulse to change the traditional form. Other public buildings are now as elusive as ghosts: mints, market-halls and centres of exchange. As with the Water Judges of Valencia, who controlled the irrigation system, much public administration was conducted in the open air for all to hear.

The Arabs were influenced by Visigothic and Byzantine decoration and used variations of the Corinthian or Composite orders bequeathed by the Romans. Their own interlace patterns evolved rapidly, but whereas crossed Romanesque

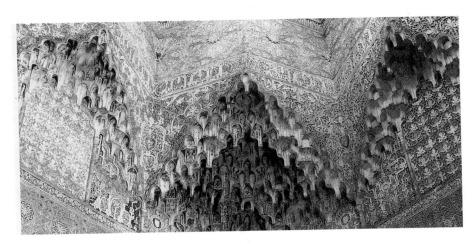

Granada, the Alhambra: *muqarnas* or stalactite dome of the Sala de los Abencerrajes.

semi-circular arches achieved the pointed Gothic style, crossed horseshoe arches created spearheads. The simple lobed arch of Syria was superseded by more elaborate forms, still to be seen in Africa, until it appeared to be ringed with fangs; however, the more complicated Almohad forms were rejected. Plaster was painted as if each room were iced and ceilings were adapted to the star-struck *muqarnas* form, best seen in the cascading domes of the Alhambra. There, vaults of interlocking pieces burst like frozen fireworks overhead.

Mozarabic architecture (that of Christians working under Muslims) was parallel in its development of Visigothic and Roman precedents but was always restrained, unlike the post-reconquest Mudéjar style which was above all the art of the brick and incorporated brilliantly glazed titles, *azulejos*, with panels of stars. A recurrent poetic feature was the window of twin-horseshoe arches sharing a central colonnette. Mudéjar towers are found all over Spain and village rivals village. The proportions are always good and these belfries can be severe except where interlace and trellis have gone to the craftsman's head, as if Rococo had arrived before its time. Some Mudéjar craftsmen survived the horrific persecutions of the early 17th century to be the forerunners of Art Nouveau and of a Mudéjar Revivalist style. Public services like Spanish Rail (RENFE) have patronized it and in Sevilla there is a spectacular shop which, with the equally spectacular Plaza de España, revives everything at once.

Sevilla: Mudéjar workmanship in the Alcázar.

SEVILLA, ANDALUCÍA

Sevilla (*Ishbiliyya*) emerges into history under the Romans, whose emperors Hadrian and Trajan were born at nearby Itálica. Vandal rule impoverished it after AD 411 until the Visigoths made it their first capital in 441. It became the Arab headquarters until overshadowed by Córdoba, but by 1031 Sevilla was once more the leading city of Andalucía. The rich countryside around it produced olive oil, figs and cereals and a fine yield of honey. Its flocks and herds were envied and its horses sought after in Europe. The citizens luxuriated in fish from both the Atlantic and the Mediterranean and travellers expatiated on the vegetables found in its markets, which were strictly regulated. Like Córdoba, Sevilla in the ninth century became a centre of silk weaving. The import trade was in Jewish hands and families had hereditary connections across Europe and Asia as far as Canton. The fine woven *tiraz* (striped silk), ceremonial robes and brocades were now produced at home. Their patterns followed traditional Byzantine forms related to those of Sassanian Iran, including the inset heraldic beast repeated along diagonals. The puritanical Almohads shut down the looms but the industry recovered. Patterns, whether sketched for wood, stone or plaster, were now based on geometry and stylized natural forms but incorporated, above all, symbols of the heavenly spheres and stars. They included inscriptive bands proclaiming the holy writ. Sevilla was also famous for metalwork such as the chased and engraved bronze on the doors of the Great Mosque.

The mansions of the rich are gone although their foundations must lie under later buildings. Traces remain in the Patio de las Banderas and the Patio del Yeso in the Alcázar. After the reconquest, the Nasrid style of the Alhambra continued to evolve in the Mudéjar style. Carpenters and gilders produced astonishing wooden ceilings which hang in dark-stained grandeur with an elaborate interlock of pieces to form domes in webbed layers and vaults of inimitable intricacy; their dark shadows give the illusion of airy ships floating upside-down in the void.

(*Opposite*) Sevilla, the Alcázar: across the Patio de las Muñecas and the Salón de los Embajadores are the apartments of María de Padilla.

19

Sevilla
1. Alcázar; 2. Casa de la Condesa de Lebrija; 3. Casa de Pilatos; 4. Hospital de la Caridad;
5. Palacio de las Dueñas;
6. Ayuntamiento;
7. Museo de Bellas Artes; 8. Puerta Macarena; 9. Torre del Oro; 10. San Salvador;
11. Cathedral; 12. La Giralda;
13. Convento de la Encarnación;
14. Convento de Santa Clara;
15. Convento de Santa Paula; 16. San Andrés; 17. San Esteban; 18. San Marcos; 19. Omnium Sanctorum; 20. Santa Ana; 21. Santa Catalina; 22. Santa María la Blanca;
23. San Isidro;
24. Santa Marina.

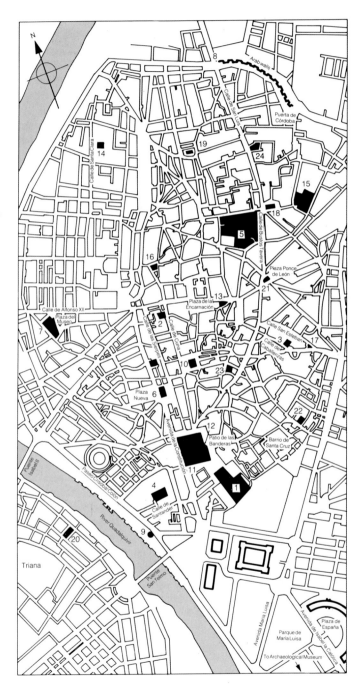

The **Barrio de Santa Cruz** was the Jewish quarter and retains the dignity of sequestered streets although punctuated by the abrasive noise of taverns. The streets on the north side of Sevilla survive and the sinuous main artery can still be followed, particularly when lit at night, all the way to the Macarena Gate: but not a trace remains of the colleges and *khans* (lodgings for merchants and centres of trade), except for one in Calle Mariana Pineda, next to the *Ayuntamiento*. Until scholars fled from the boorish Almohads and their puritanical divines, the city was enriched by the wisdom of such men as Averroës (*see* Introduction) just as it was by merchants. Sevilla was always in danger from floods but the worst flood of all was not water but the Vikings or Normans, who came up the river in 844 to slaughter and pillage. But natural floods in the early 13th century were severe and frequent, almost as if they were the allies of the Christian armies whose raids culminated in a 17-month siege and the fall of the city to Ferdinand III. Muslim attempts to recapture it merely resulted in ravage and carnage. Now the great buildings disappeared, their stones re-used to smother their foundations.

The *Alcázar* was founded as early as 712 and fortified against an unruly populace. The present austere, blind walls were built by 'Abd ar-Rahman II in the ninth century, although the ashlar gate was added a century later. Alterations were carried out after the fall of the caliphate in 1031 and by Pedro I, the Cruel. Additions and mutilations have continued ever since. Here in 1364, Pedro built the Mudéjar palace and here he killed an emir from Granada out of lust for his jewels. A great ruby eventually became the property of John of Gaunt and the Black Prince before being set in the crown of England.

Pedro obtained plasterers and carpenters from his Nasrid friend Muhammad V at Granada and his own capital, Toledo. The resulting work is Islamic, in spite of Gothic details, and follows the Islamic tradition of halls off open courts with fountains. The walls are covered in painted stucco and glazed tiles to defuse the solidity of the surfaces. Islamic columns and capitals were re-used and some purchased from Madinat az-Zahra', the Windsor of Córdoba (see p. 59). The Puerta del León (Gate of the Lion)

THE ALCÁZAR
(*Plaza del Triunfo*)

admits to the Patio de la Montería. Beyond is Pedro's palace which has a courtyard pebbled in rustic patterns. The greatly restored façade beneath deep eaves of bricks angled in the Byzantine manner is topped by a perky tower. The effect is of a palace from the famous mosaic of the church of San Vitale in Ravenna. Each wing has a kingly central arch flanked by three smaller arches like courtiers, while over the major door paired arcaded windows attend the group in the centre. The arcades were probably hung with patterned silk curtains suitably looped back. The blue and white inscription proclaims that there is no victor but Allah, but above it is a paean to Pedro, with the date of 1402 (1364 by modern reckoning). The oak and vine reliefs on the lintels are the work of craftsmen from Toledo.

The visitor enters and turns sharply. Such a blind entry had become traditional (as a draught trap if not for defence) and confronts strangers with sudden, unimagined vistas. Over the vestibule doors are elongated voussoirs as useless as a

The Patio de las Doncellas with its water, arcade and the poetic use of the vista.

mandarin's fingernails which make a nice introduction to fantasies to come. These are reached by a long hall that opens onto the **Patio de las Doncellas** (Court of the Maidens) which is the heart of the palace and which must have felt more spacious still before the ugly upper storey was imposed in the 16th century. Multi-lobed arches support façades of a network of lace-like stone and foliage in which lurk human faces besides the shields of Castile, León and Trastamara. The rhythm of three arches each side of the grand entry to a grand hall is continually satisfying. On the right is the **Salón de los Reyes Moros** (Hall of the Moorish Kings), with fine Mudéjar woodwork, a triple horseshoe arched arcade and deep alcoves for beds. The doors are remarkable because the lower panels are unrelated to the starry panels of those above. The upper patio of the harem, the **Patio de las Muñecas** (Court of the Dolls), would have been the most Islamic had a floor not been added in 1843. It is kith and kin to Madinat az-Zahra', from which the columns and capitals may have been purchased. Inset into the curtain walls are the little heads which give this patio its name. Off the main court the rooms of Pedro's mistress, the remarkable María de Padilla, are now lifeless, but the central hall is the climax of any visit. It should be approached through the 14th-century **Puerta de los Pavones** (Gate of the Peacocks); the peacocks are depicted in relief, the masterpiece of plasterers from Toledo, who inscribed their work collectively in Arabic. It makes a fitting entry to the **Salón de los Embajadores** (Ambassadors). Its triple

(*Above*) Mudéjar decoration and toothed arches in the Patio de las Doncellas.

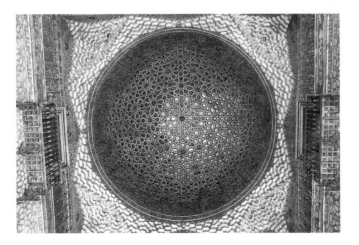

The dome of the Salón de los Embajadores is a blazing starscape.

23

horseshoe-arched arcades are sharply cut while the ornament, even deprived of colour, is so lavish that it would numb the senses were it not for the vistas beyond the arcades. Vistas are the Thousand and One Nights of Islamic architecture. The dome is starlit above subdued *muqarnas* squinches (shoulders of masonry supporting the dome, in this case interlocking woodwork producing the effect of stalactites) which catch and reflect the light. This was added in 1427 and is the work of Diego Ruiz. The tile panels run the gamut of Islamic patterns. Curved tripods, alternating up and down, cartwheel across a wall; the trellises and networks link diagonally; stars project or recede. The most elaborate plaster design is a foliate lattice inset with pine cones, some of which are crushed into thistle heads and others conjured into three-dimensional shells. There are also Gothic-framed portraits of Spanish royalty.

Alfonso XI built the **Sala de Justicia** next door to the **Patio del Yeso** (Court of Stucco), which, with its somewhat scruffy but sympathetic greenery, can only be glimpsed. The Banu Abad Ta'ifa princes who briefly enjoyed the wealth of Sevilla, living in the Alcázar after the fall of the caliphate, built this arcadia which was altered by Yusuf ibn Tashfin, the Almohad ruler, when emir between 1171–6. The court had trellised interlace over sharp-toothed arches on frail columns. Fine elliptical arches surmount entrances with paired arches: the horseshoe is here seen at its most elegant.

Beyond are the gardens and park with a basin as large as a lagoon and tiled walks. Beneath a fine Islamic blind arcade is a view into the Islamic garden given to María de Padilla. Rebuilt by Alfonso X, here is the only mark left by Ferdinand III. In the so-called *hammam* his stone vaulting is Gothic and represents a superlative vista of light and shadow reflected in still water. Everywhere else rebuilding and replanting have conquered. The gardens have a spurious Islamic atmosphere but a Muslim emir or Pedro himself would be lost, except in the vicinity of the pavilion of Charles V where there are vestiges of the orange grove of which it was said that the sun never penetrated this, the most peaceful place in Spain.

OTHER SECULAR MONUMENTS	The **Casa de la Condesa de Lebrija** (*Calle de Cuna*), begun in the 16th century, is notable for its ceilings,

especially the great wooden example installed over the staircase, a prize rescued from a palace at Marchena. The plasterwork and the *azulejo* panels are typical.

The **Casa de Pilatos** (*Calle de Caballerizas, Plaza de Pilatos*), begun in 1480, was extended over a long period with Gothic additions and less digestible Renaissance

Courtyard of the Casa de Pilatos.

intrusions. Much of the *azulejo* and plasterwork is at its best in the garden courts. The main patio is 16th-century Mudéjar at its most spectacular but it is also populated with coarse Roman statuary imported from Southern Italy but rumoured to have come from Itálica. Opinions differ over this courtyard: there are those who find that the decoration is a conglomerate in which the craftsmen have lost their way in introverted mazes. This reaction continues through other halls where the elaboration has been seen once too often. This is not true of the entrance court, which is rustically higgledy-piggledy, nor of the grand first floor terrace, whatever may be said about the pink arcades of the galleries. In the altar alcove of the chapel is an imitation Visigoth figure of the Good Shepherd. The wooden ceilings are fine examples of the late Mudéjar style. The finest is that over the grand staircase which Pontius Pilate never trod, whatever the tale that the son of this fantasia's founder, Fadrique de Rivera, told about seeing the non-existent house of Pilate on his visit to Jerusalem.

The **Hospital de la Caridad** (*Calle Temprado*) has all that is left of the shipyards established by the Muslim rulers.

The **Palacio de las Dueñas** (*Calle Espíritu Santo*) is the residence, in a quarter cherished by footpads, of the Duchess and Duke-Consort of Alba. It dates from the 15th century but was enlarged at various periods. The Mudéjar court is surrounded by elongated arches supported on elegant marble columns but the lobed decoration has become mere notching. The saloon on the upper floor has a magnificent but idiosyncratic octagonal ceiling which slopes upwards to a flat centrepiece enriched with panels round a radiant sun. There are handsome wooden doors of good traditional craftsmanship.

MUSEUMS

The **Ayuntamiento** (Town Hall) (*Plaza Nueva*) is a fine building with disparate façades housing a small Islamic collection. The **Museo Arqueológico** (Archaeological Museum) (*Parque de María Luisa, Plaza de America*) is a succulent example of Mudéjar revivalism externally. It holds a modest collection of Islamic tiles, pottery and woodwork.

The **Museo de Bellas Artes** (Fine Arts Museum) (*Plaza del Museo*) was established as early as 1828 in the former Convento de la Merced dating from the 17th century. It contains the last word in wooden ceilings with its coupled strapwork culminating in six gilded heavenly bodies set about the sun in an octagon which must be deemed the ultimate in Islamic cosmological symbolism.

The great walls of cement and rubble survived until the 1860s when they were demolished to facilitate the expansion of the city. Once 6 km (4 miles) in extent with twelve gates and 116 towers, only the section between the Córdoba and Macarena gates survives. This consists of a curtain wall with a patrol walk, seven much-restored towers and one or two ill-tempered dogs. The **Torre Blanca**, white because it was the custom to whitewash masonry, especially after a victory, is polygonal. Others are square and wear bands of interlace ornament in relief. The Almoravids added an outer wall 35 m (124 ft) beyond these ramparts, the width of the present road, like the walls of Constantinople.

THE WALLS
(*Puerta Macarena*)

In 1220 the governor, 'Abd-Allah, added an angled outwork to the city walls where they joined those of the *Alcázar* to reach the river. This was anchored by the twelve-sided **Torre del Oro** (Tower of Gold), so-called because the uppermost storey was encircled by lustre tiles. The Torre, after serving as a prison, is now the Maritime Museum. At night, for defence, it was linked by a chain to a tower on the opposite shore. Two lower storeys have survived from Islamic times but the upper floors and the lantern were rebuilt. The Muslims used uncut stone embedded in mortar in the tradition of the Almoravid bastions. In the same tradition, the rooms inside are vaulted round groined arches which form an alternating pattern of rectangles and triangles round the central stair. The windows are simple but exterior walls are decorated with blind arcading and blue and white tiles like so much Delft.

TORRE DEL ORO
(*Paseo Cristóbal Colón*)

The Torre del Oro which once defended the dockyard.

San Salvador, in the midst of the city, is built on the site of the first Umayyad Friday Mosque, founded in AD 859. It was 48.5 m (160 ft) wide and divided into seven aisles, the central one, as at Córdoba, being wider than the five on either side. This mosque became too small and the Almohad ruler Yusuf founded a successor on a grand scale, although his son was

THE FIRST GREAT MOSQUE (*Plaza del Salvador*)

San Salvador: the belfry and arches are relics of the mosque. Note how much the ground level has risen.

to restore the old one. The tower is among the oldest surviving buildings of Islamic Spain with a base 5.8 m (19 ft) square. It is mounted by a spiral stair which winds round a cylindrical newel post of its own making. The top had to be rebuilt after the earthquake of 1395. The patio retains its old form although the ground level has risen. Only a few low arches and the base of the minaret remain. The beautiful doorknockers are conserved in the sacristy.

| THE CATHEDRAL AND LA GIRALDA | The second great mosque was built in 1172 and converted to Christian use in 1248. Later it was torn down and the present Santa María de la Sede was erected between 1402 and 1506; it is still the largest Gothic cathedral. The minaret and part of the Patio de los Naranjos remain. On the north |

side an enclosing wall of fired brick with some areas covered in elegant plasterwork in relief survives as do the paths to the ablution fountains, which are Visigothic in origin. The 19 horseshoe arches of two arcades are Islamic. The mosque had been some 150 × 100 m (495 × 330 ft) in extent and had 17 pillared aisles, the central aisle wider than the rest. Outside were phalanxes of lofty horseshoe blind arcades and rectangular buttresses. No Almohad felt respect for Córdoba, yet, in the Córdoban manner, the skyline of the patio is castellated with toothed merlons. The Almohad **Puerta del Perdón** (Gate of Absolution) has stretches of Almohad wall on either side and doors with 12th-century Arabic inscriptions on bronze panels as well as sumptuously pierced knockers.

A second gate is the **Puerta del Oriente** (East Gate). Inside is the **Puerta del Lagarto** (Door of the Crocodile). This creature was a gift — among other more attractive items, one might suppose — sent by the Sultan of Egypt when he asked for the hand of a daughter of Alfonso X in 1263. The gate is obscured by the Mudéjar entrance to the **Capilla de Nuestra Señora de la Granada**, which has a fine ceiling and a fistful of Visigothic capitals. The patio is endowed with a sad beauty due to its unspoilt proportions and orange trees whose fruit glow 'in a green night' and were, as one traveller remarked, destined to become Oxford marmalade. Inside the cathedral is the **Capilla de San Fernando**, the saint-king. It is necessary to kneel to see the three incompar-

The bronze doors of the Puerta del Perdón which leads to the Patio de los Naranjos.

able pieces of calligraphy in his honour in Latin, Hebrew and Arabic.

The grandest of minarets, **La Giralda** is only rivalled by its parent, the Kutubiyya of Marrakesh, founded by the Almohads, who lasted so briefly once their religious mania was civilized. It still dominates the heart of Sevilla but the cumbrous belfry on top, added between 1520 and 1568 by Hernán Ruiz, should be disregarded. The 4 m (13 ft)-high figure of Faith is a weathervane, or *Giraldilla*. La Giralda was begun in 1184 by the master mason Ahmad ibn Basi on deep ashlar foundations but above ground was built of re-used stone and finally completed in brick. The work was achieved by Abu Yusuf Ya'qub, the architect's apprentice and successor, who finished the tower in 1198. From the base, over 16 m (53 ft) square, the tower rises round a brick core to about 50 m (164 ft) and contains seven rooms, in deference to the seven heavenly bodies. There are no stairs, only gently sloping ramps. Externally each face is divided into three sections to form a series of large, geometrically decorated panels in shallow relief. Within these are traditional double windows divided by a slim column and blind arcading. It is the proportion of each section in relation to the bare walling that achieves serenity and balance only ruffled by later consoled balconies.

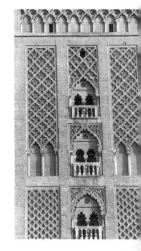

A detail of the delicate tracery on La Giralda.

In the **Convento de la Encarnación** (*Plaza de la Encarnación*) the presbytery was a part of a mosque of which some windows survive on the outside wall.

The **Convento de Santa Clara** (*Calle de Santa Clara*) is the nunnery church begun in the 15th century in the Mudéjar-Gothic style and has a wooden ceiling of distinction.

The **Convento de Santa Paula** (*Calle de Santa Paula*) hides a little octagonal Mudéjar cloister and some other scraps from the period within the church.

Omnium Sanctorum (*Calle de la Feria*) has a porch which is a good example of one Mudéjar style of the 13th century. The belfry is a shrivelled version of the top of La Giralda.

San Andrés (*Plaza de San Andrés*) only preserves the husk of the Mudéjar-Gothic church.

San Esteban (*Calle de San Esteban*) dating from *c.*1400, preserves a panel of lobed arches in the Almohad tradition. Three fine ceilings and excellent *azulejos* enrich the interior.

MUDÉJAR CONVENTS AND CHURCHES

(*Opposite*) La Giralda: the original minaret is surmounted by the Christian belfry.

San Isidoro (*Calle de San Isidoro*) is a 14th-century church with a Mudéjar doorway and notable interlace decoration on the ceiling.

San Marcos (*Plaza de San Marcos*) was a fourth-century Roman monument resurrected in about 1350. A superb building, it has noble horseshoe arches, handsomely proportioned nave and aisles but with some Gothic vaulting and polyglot doors in a hotchpotch of styles. It stands in a rough quarter and was purged by fire during the Civil War, which accounts for the uncluttered *gravitas* of the interior, the most moving in Sevilla. The sensitive Mudéjar minaret has elegant brickwork and is enriched at the top with brick eaves; the handsome turret is closer to a minaret in form than to a belfry.

Santa Ana (*Calle de la Pureza*) Triana, was built by Alfonso X in 1280 but rebuilt in the 14th century. Worse, in 1971 it was deprived of its plaster in order to indecently expose the brick beneath.

Santa Catalina (*Plaza Ponce de León*) was a mosque which was rebuilt as a church in the 14th century in Mudéjar style and then distorted later. The simple apses are austere brickwork and the bell tower on the Almohad minaret base is a fine example of Mudéjar at its most severe.

Santa María la Blanca (*Calle de Santa María la Blanca*) was built in 1391 on the site of a synagogue and then rebuilt in the 17th century, retaining a Mudéjar doorway and one or two Visigoth capitals.

Santa Marina (*Calle de San Luis*) has a fine ceiling; the minaret was converted into a belfry.

OTHER SITES
NEAR SEVILLA

ALANIS

Apart from traces of fortifications there is no surviving Islamic building, but the spirit lingers on with fine examples of Mudéjar craftsmanship.

ALCALÁ DE GUADAIRA

This impressive fortress stands aloof above the town, murky river and burnt omelette of a plain. The square keep built after the reconquest and the long curtain walls were admired by Washington Irving. La Mora was one of the finest Almohad castles and its austerity is symbolic of their outlook. It has Visigoth and Roman antecedents and shows how military engineering is international. The castle is gutted and unconserved, the raw haunt of feckless youths and melancholia. It is difficult to imagine Ferdinand III lodging here in the 13th century with any pleasure other than a sense of security, which today would be false. With underground corn stores and several cisterns, the fortress was provisioned against the long siege which led to its surrender in 1246. The town was nicknamed Alcalá de los Panaderos (Bakers) because it supplied Sevilla with bread. Several old corn mills are recognizable on the slopes on both sides of the river. The church of **San Miguel** retains traces of its Muslim past.

ARACENA
The formidable fortress was captured by the Knights Templar who greatly extended the work of the Almohads. The late 13th-century church of **Nuestra Señora de los Dolores** was built on the site of the mosque and retains the handsome brick Torre Ariosa as a belfry.

BOLULLOS DE LA MITACIÓN
Five km (3 miles) outside the town is the **Ermita Cuatrohab-itant** with a fine 12th-century minaret and the original *mihrab* niche, suitably whitewashed.

CARMONA (*Karmūna*)
The Arabs took the town as early as AD 712. They enlarged the castle on the escarpment. They also walled the town with stone and erected an arsenal and a Friday mosque (the major mosque of a city) which had arches carried on marble columns. **Santa María Mayor** was built on the site and if viewed from the castle, now a Parador (state-run hotel), the form of the lost mosque may be discerned, an effect enhanced by a tiled tower above the crossing. The church retains the patio of orange trees and horseshoe arches.

Carmona overlooks fertile meadows and fields of barley and wheat. It had famous limestone quarries, excellent clay, and its garnets were sought after because of the purity of their fire. The region was populated by Berbers and so became a centre of unrest. Early in Islamic history in Spain an avenging mission was sent by the Abbasid caliph, who had slaughtered the Umayyad family, to besiege 'Abd ar-Rahman I, here in Carmona. They were fanatical Yemenis fired by jealousy of the young emir's Syrian henchmen, but

The Islamic gateway
of the Alcázar de
Arriba, Carmona.

after two futile months they withdrew. In the ninth century frequent uprisings centred on the town and in 844 refugees fled there to escape the merciless Vikings. In the 11th century the Almoravids strengthened the castle but Castilian raiders savaged the farms in the 13th century until Ferdinand III took the city in 1247. The Roman Puerta de Sevilla was rebuilt by the Arabs as a fort, the **Alcázar de Abajo**. The Plaza de San Fernando is surrounded by fine Mudéjar houses which include the **Cabildo Antiguo**, the old Council House, from the 15th century, while **San Felipe** and **Santiago** are Mudéjar churches, the former with a noble ceiling and the other with interesting brickwork. The old Córdoba road leads to a five-arched Roman bridge, above which is the **Alcázar de Arriba** (the 'Castle Above' as opposed to that 'Below' — *Abajo*). Pedro I transformed this Almohad fortress into a palace of which nothing remains.

ÉCIJA (*Istidji*)
The town had deep Iberian roots. Neither intruders from Carthage nor the Visigoths left any trace except, perhaps, for bones, since Rodrigo may have been defeated and buried here. During the Ta'ifa Kings period, the Berber Zirids made Écija and Jaén their citadels but Andalucían hostility to these newcomers from North Africa alarmed their emir. He removed himself to the impregnable heights of Granada where his successors held out briefly until after a pogrom

they gave way to the Nasrids. Here Ferdinand set up his base before the final assault on Granada, letting the inhabitants remain until their fractiousness resulted in their expulsion. The Mozarab subjects had previously rebelled against the caliph and it had become the cursed city of the Umayyads. Then it was that the bridge and town were razed to the ground, somewhat impulsively, since their strategic importance meant that they had to be rebuilt. No one in their senses would live there and the heat which swaddles the town may explain its history. Fortress, towers and gates have Islamic foundations but belong to several periods. Indeed, towers, some sparkling with *azulejos*, are so numerous that the town was known as the Ciudad de las Torres.

GUADALCANAL
Of the three Mudéjar churches, **San Sebastián** is the finest. **La Asunción** and **Santa Ana** are modest and restored. Traces of Arab walls remain, imagination permitting.

HUELVA
The town, damaged in the Lisbon earthquake of 1755, recovered because its wealth was earned from the sea. It is now a cement centre and has on occasion a moonlike appearance. On the outskirts is a rare example of a Muslim aqueduct. **San Pedro** was built out of a mosque of which traces may be found. The sanctuary of **Nuestra Señora de la Cinta** (Our Lady of the Girdle) has noble ceilings. The famous monastery of **La Rábida** on the romantic estuary of the Río Tinto has a Mudéjar cloister and a noteworthy ceiling over the nave of the church. It is the cork forests, however, which could be thought to be the finest architecture in this extremity of Spain.

LEBRIJA
The walls and castle were Almohad but much repaired and altered. **Santa María** was resurrected from the site of an Almohad mosque and has a bell-tower which may have begun as a minaret. Inside the church the two aisles are divided by handsome horseshoe arches while the four domes are remarkable.

MOGUER
Nuestra Señora de Granada has a restrained copy of La

Giralda for its bell-tower while the 14th-century **Convento de Santa Clara** in the Mudéjar style houses *azulejos* in choir and chapter-house.

MORÓN DE LA FRONTERA

The town is dominated by a ruined **Alcázar** which has ruined Roman antecedents. The **Convento de los Mínimos** has an excellent wooden ceiling while **San Miguel** has a version of La Giralda for its bell-tower.

NIEBLA (Nr Huelva)

Niebla was the see of a Visigoth bishop and remained largely Christian under Muslim rule. The town was the centre of the saffron and the raisin trades but its strategic importance above the road from Portugal was the reason for its magnificent fortifications rising above river and eucalyptus trees. Shorn as stretches of the walls have been, they enclose the Almohad town, complete with 46 towers and four gates and offer a spectacular aspect as they curve above the Roman bridge where Muslim repairs are plain to see. It is alleged that the Río Tinto (Red River) was so called because of the reflection of these walls. The *albarrani* tower or salient is noteworthy, as is the **Puerta del Agua** (Water Gate), a perfect example of a bent entrance besides being trimly built of cut stone with a horseshoe arch springing from only a few feet above the middle of the opening. When the land dips the height of the walls is maintained. Both the **Puerta del Buey** (Gate of the Ox) and the **Puerta de Socorro** (Rescue Gate) have horseshoe arches. More typically Umayyad is the re-use of ashlar blocks for footings and at the corners of towers, with rough-hewn stones between. So daunting were the fortifications that Alfonso X had to wait six months before Niebla surrendered in 1262. The *Alcazaba* is in ruins.

The church of **Santa María de la Granada** is exceptionally beautiful. The outer gate, due to the winding of the former street, is happily set at an angle to the irregular courtyard with its broad arcade of horseshoe arches, blind across the church wall. When the restored door is opened only a glimpse may be caught of the interior beyond the 11-lobed brick arch which springs from robust foliate capitals borne by two marble columns. Soft pink brick suffuses the interior with a gentle shade and the modest building astonishes by the loftiness of the nave and the drama of its

Niebla: a blind entrance exposing an enemy to attack from above could be the precursor of the *albarrani* tower.

elegant arches. The Gothic stone arches are incongruous in the midst of warm clay. A gilded statuette is set inside the former *mihrab* niche which lies beyond another horseshoe arch supported on colonnettes. This was a Mozarabic church before it was converted into a mosque in Almohad times. The minaret is austere in conformity with Almohad severity in spite of coupled windows two-thirds of the way up to where the bells now hang. The rear of the church shows the complexity of its history with a jumble of jostling roofscapes.

The modern town has nothing to do with the pretty white world of Andalucía. As long as the morning mist veils it, a huge fortress of a factory with chimneys for towers can be seen in the imagination as a modern *Alcázar*.

Niebla: looking across the patio of Santa María de la Granda.

SANLÚCAR LA MAYOR
This white town is unrelated to nearby Niebla. Little remains of the *Alcázar*, while the Almohad mosque became a Mudéjar church immediately after the reconquest, preserving horseshoe arches and gaining a grand wooden ceiling. There is a curious cutting-away of the plaster round the windows and over the main door where there remains a pair of Islamic windows within a horseshoe arch, itself contained within a large circle. This may have been intended to become a rose window, for a smaller one above the secondary door is made up of five petals. It is set above a horseshoe arch of stone within a 15-lobed brick arch which loops neatly at its crest. **San Pedro** nearby is so unyielding in its appearance as to assert Almohad ancestry. Its broad minaret, which looks so bulky from afar, shrinks on approach to its garden setting. The Islamic **Puerta del Sol** is restored.

VILLALBA DEL ALCOR
Alcor means a hill and so it is. **San Bartolomé** was built across the old mosque in order to face east. The minaret was converted into the bell-tower and horseshoe arches survive.

ZAHARA DE LOS MEMBRILLOS (of the Quinces)
The town was guarded by a Muslim fortress. The pink stone keep is set on a spur of rock which could have been made to measure, since the summit is a perfect base for the cube of the *Alcázar*. Curtain walls were superfluous. The town also has a restored Muslim bridge.

CÓRDOBA, ANDALUCÍA

Córdoba (*Qurtubat al-Wadi al-Kabir* — Córdoba of the Great River, or the Guadalquivir) is built on an expansive plateau, Los Pedroches, which is bounded by the Sierra Morena. The geographer al-Idrisi called it a meadow of oaks. The rich terrain is watered by the Guadalquivir, which was formerly navigable from the sea, and cooled by winds iced as they crossed the snow-capped Sierra Nevada. The province prospered after the second Punic War to be annexed by Rome in 152 BC. It foolishly took the side of Pompey against Julius Caesar, who slaughtered droves of the citizens in 49 BC for making so crass a political mistake. It recovered, as cities on fine sites do, only to be devastated by the Visigoths early in the fifth century AD. It was recovered by the resurgent Byzantine Empire but retaken by the Visigoths under King Leovigild in 571. Prosperity shrivelled under their incompetent rule and the city was close to ruin when occupied by a lieutenant of the Islamic general Tariq in the summer of 711. Córdoba was the base from which the invaders were to conquer most of Spain and cross the Pyrenees.

In 711, 400 Córdoban stalwarts, fancifully dubbed knights by later wishful thinking, held out in the fortified church of San Ancisio until in October they were too weak from hunger and pestilence to draw a sword and were forced to surrender. The remnants of Córdoba's elite families awaited massacre but were treated magnanimously. The clergy remained under their bishop or metropolitan, so often the only educated leader. The inevitable poll tax was imposed on Christian and Jewish households. Little by little between 712 and the mid-century the city recovered until **'Abd ar-Rahman I** made it the capital of al-Andalus. The walls were restored and so were harbour and bridge. It is alleged that the first known Muslim cemetery in Spain was laid out there. But the outstanding event was the building of the first Friday Mosque in al-Andalus. From then on Córdoba was indeed the capital. The mosque is still known as **La Mezquita** and 'Abd ar-Rahman was to boast that it was the Ka'ba of the

(*Opposite*) Córdoba, La Mezquita: typical doorway of al-Hakam's reign.

West (the Ka'ba being the renowned black stone that fell from Heaven to be set in the modest hall in the heart of the courtyard mosque of Mecca). The erection of a mosque large enough to unite all the townspeople in prayer at noon each Friday was a shrewd and confident political act which helped to unite 'Abd ar-Rahman's dominions. It was also intended to reduce the lure of magnetic monuments such as the Dome of the Rock in Jerusalem and the Great Mosque at Damascus, which were in the hands of the Abbasids, enemies of the Umayyads. Once the emir took up residence in the *Alcázar* in 766, nothing could frustrate the growth of the city and its fabulous prosperity.

'Abd ar-Rahman did face rebellions, however: a Berber revolt seemed dangerous when the rebels sought help from Charlemagne, and further troubles lay ahead: when 'Abd ar-Rahman's grandson, **al-Hakam I**, succeeded in 794 there was another revolt. The death of the monarch is a dangerous moment for any hereditary ruling family; this was particularly true of Islamic dynasties because there was no rule of primogeniture, only a tribal tradition that a family selected the ablest male as their chief. Al-Hakam's rights were challenged by his uncle, Sulayman, who attacked the city. There was no popular rising and the upstart fled to Écija where his hotchpotch army was defeated again. Hunted from crag to crag and hamlet to hamlet as if a bandit, he fought until his inevitable capture and execution.

However on 16 January 929, perhaps the greatest Muslim ruler, Emir **'Abd ar-Rahman III** was powerful enough to proclaim himself caliph, or political successor of the Prophet, and there was nothing that the caliph in Baghdad could do. The authority of his Córdoban rival extended through the Maghrib and gave his new status the aura of an office created by Muhammad. This strengthening was reflected in the enlarged grandeur of the mosque and the even greater prosperity of the capital. Echoes of this grandeur remain in the quarter around La Mezquita, for it is typical of a Muslim town of small palaces built round watered courtyards, and to explore these streets is to meet with unexpected pleasures: glimpses through open doors (which would have been shut in Muslim times) reveal cool, tiled and flower-filled patios. Elsewhere the churches built on the sites of mosques have former minarets as bell-towers. There was nothing inherently

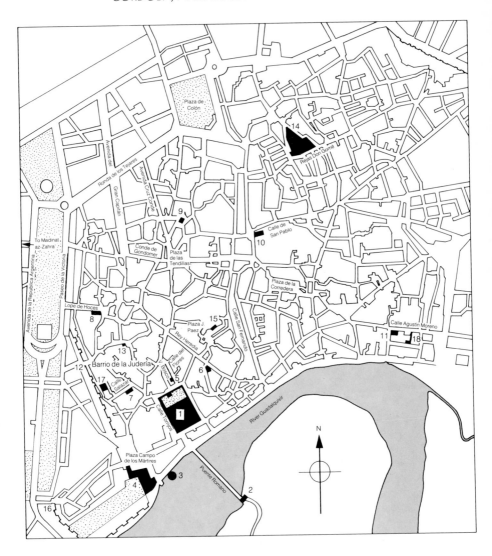

sacred about the tower from which the call to prayer was issued, so it was permissible to adapt it, since it was devoid of any sectarian overtone. Minarets were, however, a political statement of the power of a dynasty; in Córdoba most echoed Syrian Umayyad influence. The city was alleged to have 500 mosques, which, if true, must have included *mihrab* alcoves in private houses.

From the first the emir had a seat of government in the

country outside Córdoba (now disappeared), but **'Abd ar-Rahman III** founded a new constellation of palace and official buildings at **Madinat az-Zahra'**, 6 km (4 miles) outside the walls, an Islamic Versailles (see p. 59). Cornfields and vineyards, olive and orange groves and orchards produced abundant crops and the raising of cattle, bulls and thoroughbred horses was highly profitable. Flocks of sheep proliferated across the Sierras in summer and the plains in winter. All prices were regulated by the market court which not only controlled profits but the exact place where a commodity might be sold. (The *Qadi*, justice of the city, was chosen from among the professors in Madina in Arabia — the greatest university in Islam and the place where Muhammad was buried — because they were renowned for their honesty, piety and, above all, inflexibility.) Córdoba had a plethora of skilled craftsmen and international trade flourished. By the ninth century sericulture was established, as well as in Sevilla and Almería. Leather became the product for which Córdoba was most renowned and from its name the word cordwainer evolved. At some point after 850 the art of crystal was discovered in the glass workshops of Córdoba. Another skill was that of inlaid metalwork, depicting magic animals in bronze and iron; this was to be surpassed by yet finer work in silver or gold inlay. Silver and gold thread was spun for brocades, and from this activity filigree work developed. Silver was mined in the Sierra Morena (which was so sparsely populated that its lonely shepherds were said to have lost the power of speech). Gold was at first brought from Italy at extortionate prices but under the Almohads, who ruled all north-west Africa, it crossed the desert from Ghana to Marrakesh and entered Spain after passing through the great trading city of Sijilmasa; this had, since the eighth century, been the emporium of both the trade in gold and in that more necessary commodity, salt. Trade led to converts, and the gold coin of Ghadanes was restamped to show conversion to Islam, while a black emir received a Qu'ran from the caliph in Córdoba as an accession gift.

Thus Córdoba became an entrepôt for all the luxuries of the East and West, from parchment, perfumes, drugs, spices and slippers to singers, dancers and exotic bedfellows. But its elite had intellectual as well as epicurean tastes: a passion for books caused from 70,000 to 80,000 bound volumes to be produced each year. For most of these, cheaper paper had to be brought from Játiva, for demand far outran local high-quality production, especially when a caliph built up a collection of 400,000 books, all catalogued and surely constituting the largest library in the medieval world; and yet one has no idea where these acres of learning were stored. Some shops employed as many as 170 women to copy manuscripts, a different world from that of monks copying in the monastery libraries of the West. There were women bibliophiles and at least one noble blue-stocking preferred the company of her library to the bed of a husband. It is not surprising that there were also women poets, the best known of whom was Safiyya of Sevilla.

The Umayyad court was the most splendid in Europe: a haven for philosophers, poets and artists, mathematicians and astronomers. The city had been the birthplace of Seneca and Lucan and now it was the cradle of Ibn Rushd, known as Averroës (1126–1198), and the great Jewish philosopher and physician Maimonides (1135–1204) (see Introduction). Other ornaments of the court included Ziryab, lured from Baghdad. He was the musician who added the fifth string to the lute, but was much more besides: arbiter of fashion and recipes, he was among the first intellectuals to believe cooking to be both an art and a serious science. He had a splendid eye for materials and for colour, just as he had a palate as refined as any since. He set standards of refinement in deportment and table manners and established the order of the courses, from soup to sweetmeats, instead of tables being overwhelmed by an array of dishes all served at once. As if this were insufficient, he invented toothbrushes and toothpaste. He was also a powerful minister.

There can be no doubt that the tenth century was a golden age for the wealthiest city in the West — a city awake with street lighting which extended social and intellectual life long after sunset when towns elsewhere were moribund. The decline in the 11th century was due to deeply destructive political enmities between local citizens, including Berbers, Jews and Mozarabs, with each group in its own ark, so to speak. The geography was divisive and the Caliphate disintegrated into 30 or more trivial lordships, about 20 of which had moments of importance under one or the other despot from the military or the landed classes. While the

Jews maintained their unmistakable identity, the Mozarabs or Christians accepted so many Muslim customs that 'nothing seems but what is not'. There were also genuine or opportunist converts to Islam, while another important faction was the rootless slave household of the ruler. These fans of this or that competing interest, hooded by their jealousies, betrayed Córdoba to the Almohads. As early as 1236 Ferdinand III of Castile found Córdoba an easy conquest. Manufacture and prosperity dried up as if it were dew in the desert, the population dwindled and the mill-wheels ceased to turn. The core of the town survived — and one immortal monument.

LA MEZQUITA

The most moving hour at which to enter the great mosque for the first time is shortly after dawn when nobody disturbs the shadows which lie like the ladder of Jacob across the stone floor. A black-coated priest may hasten between the columns: still an intruder in a metaphysical world beyond his experience. The Emperor Charles V, who never gave the order, was appalled by the transformation of the mosque into a cathedral in the 16th century, and the archbishop had good reason to regret his responsibility for the deed. An elephantine structure was to rise in the heart of the magic vistas as if intentionally seeking to be disproportionately destructive. When he came upon this desecration, the emperor damningly remarked that the choir and sanctuary were commonplace: La Mezquita had been unique. Fortunately, here and there the eye can avoid the damage done, but the most extraordinary of the diagonal visions are gone for ever.

It may be asked why simple tiers of columns should prove to be great architecture. The building grew over a period of 200 years, its columns mostly borrowed from ruins. Legend claims that some may have been spoils from Narbonne or Nîmes, and others may have been sent by the emperor in Constantinople, in particular the porphyry examples which were no longer quarried, although they could have been found at Itálica near Sevilla. The donor in Byzantium was not Leo IV as some have claimed, since he was dead by 780, but would have been Constantine VI. A full study of the quarries from which they came originally has yet to be made.

Columns are the mean on which all measurements

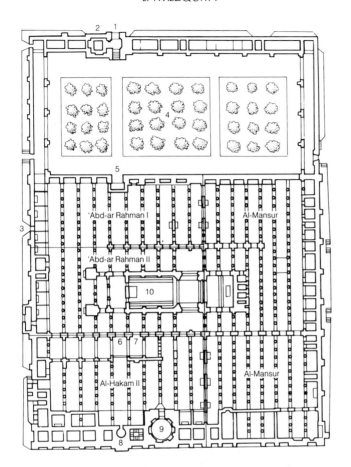

La Mezquita
1. Puerta del Perdón;
2. bell tower;
3. Puerta de San Esteban; 4. Patio de los Naranjos;
5. Puerta de las Palmas; 6. Capilla Villaviciosa;
7. Capilla Real;
8. *mihrab*; 9. sacristy;
10. cathedral.

depend — whatever the architectural style — when monoliths form the basis of all supports. Their height and width determine the weight that may be carried and also the span between them, since a column set too far apart from its mate will buckle. By the beginning of the Christian era, the Roman quarries had adopted standard measures leading to a certain uniformity in the proportions of marble units of all kinds. It follows that few buildings in Roman or Byzantine times began before the necessary columns had been assembled, since without them the final form of the building could not be conceived. What is striking about La Mezquita is that the ceilings, which are about 13 m (39 ft) high, were loftier than any easily available column could reach, which suggests that all were *spoglia* (material taken from ruins to

be re-used), and none was mint-cut. The problem was solved by placing one arch on top of another, either by hoisting a column on top of another column or by raising a pier. Before so many were obliterated by the choir and Capilla Mayor, there were probably some 850 or more columns in all, divided among the 29 east-west and 19 north-south aisles. (This figure would include those inset into the walls.) Today barely half of them are extant, but people still talk of 1,000 columns — a proper tribute to an effect like that achieved by Velázquez who, with some 29 spears, gave an impression of a great army in the background of *The Surrender in Breda* in the Prado Museum. Be that as it may; much, as always with great buildings, is in doubt. The columns are set in measured rows as orderly as conifers in a plantation but they double up one above the other in a manner unknown to tree or branch. While semi-circular arches predominate, many take a horseshoe form with that extension to the half-circle which has no structural purpose but which delights the eye. Others, related to the *mihrabs* and their flanking rooms, are not merely trefoil but multifoil. What is absent is the mildly pointed arch common to Islamic architecture elsewhere.

La Mezquita's elaborate and dramatic arches may or may not be related to those of North Africa and the arcadias of Morocco. Modestly lobed arches were common to Abbasid buildings and were sensitively used in the tenth-century Cairene mosque of Ibn Tulun. Such arches were a characteristic element of the elaborate decoration so prevalent in Islamic Spain, which reached its ultimate form in the *muqarnas* domes of Nasrid Granada. The arches of La Mezquita, even when inverted to add a fresh dimension to their agility, chiefly conform to the dimensions of the sober hemispheres and so are not out of step. It is this measured relationship which is the secret of the beauty of this building, the marvel of kings and simple travellers alike for more than 1,000 years. Changes in form interrupt the monotony of the sequences without disturbing the harmony: the one wider aisle leading to the *mihrab* is an important break with the subliminal effect of accentuating the harmony.

The geometric designs were familiar in Samarra' and Fatimid Egypt, together with the elementary interlace of the Anatolian Seljuqs. Pine cones, still popular in the form of the local pine-kernel marzipan, were symbols much used by the

(*Opposite*) The interior of La Mezquita, Córdoba.

47

The Patio de los Naranjos and the belfry of La Mezquita which encases the minaret.

Visigoths. Such decoration is fine but it is only in the splendour of the *mihrab* chamber that it becomes a true partner and not subordinate to structural form. Tranquillity and restrained grandeur are not the result of chance, as one realizes at once on stepping out into the **Patio de los Naranjos** to find that the orange trees continue the rhythms of the interior aisles. In the last extension to the mosque made before the fall of the Caliphate there is one more strange break, where three columns appear in the place of two and the normal void between upper and lower arch is filled in with something akin to a grindstone. The function of this square area is not clear but perhaps it was built to take a teacher's chair. This break in the rhythm can easily pass unnoticed, as was perhaps intended.

Crowds amble about the building all day and thus it is as it was intended it should be, full of life and movement. Today one can only imagine the flickering of oil lamps and candles that would have brought the mosaics — silver and gold clasped in glass — to life, unlike the dull hum of electricity. Austere intervals, essential to a place of meditation, contrast with decorative riches such as the *mihrab* tiles, but no longer with the capitals, once gloriously gilded.

If, in this tranquil, twilight world, the visitor standing amidst rows of columns stretching almost out of sight has the sensation of being in the depths of a forest, it would not be inappropriate: the forest *was* in the ceilings, for the pines from which they were constructed were dragged from the great mountain forests of the north in long ox wagons for week after week. Mainly replaced by plaster vaults, the timber ceilings that remain are largely reproductions copied from surviving beams of the original ceilings. It was to support the hidden baulks and beams that the arches stood; these in turn supported the ridges of tiled roofing that run from north to south, their gutters ending in large spouts which, until the cathedral rose up like a floating dock to dominate them, articulated the façades in measured unity.

La Mezquita reveals a logical growth which is not difficult to understand. The earliest building is easily traced once one discards improbabilities such as the mythical incorporation of a wall of the Visigothic church, which must have been modest in size. That the old foundations were made use of, however, is suggested by the misalignment of the *mihrab*, which does not point directly towards Mecca. The church itself could have been built on the site of the Temple of Janus since it was opposite the Roman headquarters and because two inscriptions have been found in the mosque. The Roman palace was to be the rebuilt residence of the emir when he was not ruling from the country, and it eventually became the palace of the archbishop after the reconquest. The growth in the Muslim population made sharing the Christian church impossible, and after haggling 'Abd ar-Rahman was able to purchase and demolish it in 786 and complete his mosque in one year. It was a pillared hall opening on to its court in the Umayyad tradition — so grand at Damascus and so moving at Qayrawan in Tunisia — which homesickness perhaps prompted the emir to recreate here. (Creswell, the greatest of British historians of Islamic architecture, records his poem to a lonely palm tree, one of the first to be brought to Spain, in which he compares his exile with that of the tree, for both were far from home.) He employed a Syrian architect, but it is curious that the arcades were built perpendicular to the back wall for which the only precedent was the Aqsa Mosque at Jerusalem, where the gable roofing is also similar. The columns may dominate but the arches, composed of white marble segments with carefully tapered red brick segments between them, fill the interior with colour in the Syrian manner. The double arches were totally new, as was the stilting of some of the upper arches, which are fixed like clamps to the shoulders of the arch below. The lower arch itself has nothing to support but is a half-circle etched in space. Later it would develop ornamental lobes and end up as fantastic strapwork, but whatever form it took it was more a tie-beam than an arch. It stopped the spreading of the double load and the fall of the columns beneath. The scholar Gómez-Moreno suggested that this concept, of an acrobat riding upon his partner's shoulders, was derived from triple-arched Roman aqueducts such as the one at Mérida, where the arches may be tie-beams but the structure of burly piers hardly appears to need tethering like an arcade. Both he and Creswell believed that it is likely that the tiers of La Mezquita were a new solution forced upon the builder.

Within 50 years prosperity resulted in a greatly increased population and 'Abd ar-Rahman II added five aisles to the south, which required 80 new columns. This area is now sadly mutilated by the choir of the cathedral. The *mihrab* had also to be moved south and the enlarged mosque formed a square. This new *mihrab* with its multi-toothed elaborate arches is now the domed **Capilla Villaviciosa**, its squinches and arcades only subordinate to those of the present *mihrab*. The richly ornamented room beside it served as the *maqsura* or royal enclosure, constructed because the emir did not wish those at prayer to rise in respect when he entered the mosque. It is here that the fine columns of the original *mihrab* can be seen and that the undulations of the cusped arches and inverted arches interrupt the march of marble towards the present great *mihrab*. This was built when al-Hakam II extended the mosque southwards yet again in 964. The brand new *mihrab* formed a separate room in place of the more modest

La Mezquita: The Capilla Villaviciosa, built as the *mihrab* in the ninth century.

niche of old. The interior is brilliant with the reflected light from the mosaics, for the Byzantine emperor sent tesserae of red, green, silver and gold to be outlined in white and black, together with master craftsmen to install them. They created verdant patterns from nature in the Byzantine canon, and noble inscriptions were doubtless carefully copied from the designs of leading Arab calligraphers. The walls are corseted in blind arcading riding from coupled column to coupled column, lobed at the centre and with windows above. From these rises the ribbed dome, seemingly supported by an eight-pointed star, made by ribs which are the sides of two squares, one turned by 45 degrees across the other. The eight arches which form the star leapfrog across

La Mezquita: the *mihrab* chamber's ribbed dome is supported by leaping arches.

each other to create sharply pointed arches which cut across the corners of the square room. The squinches project curiously blatantly. The ribs have no structural importance but their star form captured the imagination of the West, was copied all over Christian Spain and eventually reached as far as Turin and the Church of San Lorenzo. The *mihrab* dome was once believed to have been cut out of one immense block of marble and, according to legend, hoisted into place in June 965 while all the onlookers held their breath. Less amazingly, it is in fact made of plaster. As with every dome, it is a triumphant symbol of the Divine. The magnificent columns of the old *mihrab* were in some cases re-erected in the new and the decoration was completed apace within six months.

In al-Hakam's reign the use of brick with stone, geometric patterns for their own sake and coloured mosaic all reflect Byzantine influence. The emergence of shells, with all their symbolism of womb and haven, indicates a tentative change from the dominant star motif.

The lobed arches of the converted Capilla de San Fernando which stand on the heads of the double columns below, along with the upper strata of triple colonnettes is less aesthetic than amazing. The addition of 14 aisles nearly doubled the area of the prayer hall but it meant that the mosque was deeper than it was broad. The court had been deepened in preparation for this by 'Abd ar-Rahman III so that the work of father and son must be seen as a single campaign. Whether the length disturbed al-Mansur or whether there was another increase in population, he added eight longitudinal aisles to the east flank because the river was dangerously close to the south side and to move the *mihrab* again was unthinkable. The west side was blocked by the palace and so the east side was the only possible place, although it involved the demolition of many valuable properties and the payment of costly compensation.

The original form of La Mezquita was restored, along with the tradition that as many as possible of the faithful who arrived early should be honoured by a place in the first rank. The façade on to the patio was extended in the old manner, bringing the total number of horseshoe arches to 17, each 4 m (13 ft) in width. No new grand door could be made if it were to be aligned with the *mihrab* and so the extension feels slightly apart, as if it were a waiting-room. A huge cistern was sunk into the patio, which was enclosed by a castellated and merloned wall.

The even spacing of the outward buttresses survives but only one of the doorways. An inscription above the **Puerta de San Esteban** gives the date as 855. The red and white decorations, windows and blind arcading of the doors and other areas between the buttresses and the striking drain-spouts form hanging ornamental carpets along the flanks of the monument. The **Puerta del Perdón**, the main entrance to the patio and possibly the least used, absolution or no absolution, has towers each side of its Mudéjar lobed arches and 14th-century doors and knockers. Reliefs on the inside wall of the belfry depict the lost minaret, which is sheathed inside the present tower. There is evidence that it had twin stairways which rose independently until the belfry faltered under the weight of additional masonry and the bells when struck by the great storm of 1589. By 1618 it was so unstable that it was encased in masonry 1.5 m (5 ft) thick and lost its former elegance. It is a vantage point from which to study the roofscape of La Mezquita and the trim heads of the orange trees in the patio. The Gothic arcades were erected after the reconquest. The **Puerta de las Palmas**, for there are palms by this door, which was the principal entrance to the prayer-hall, is a Mudéjar replacement. What have not changed are the measurements of the building which, with its patio, runs approximately 178 m (585 ft) from north to south and 125 m (410 ft) from east to west to make a total area of 22,250 sq m (26,500 sq yd). Additions after the reconquest include the **Capilla Real** ensconced by Alfonso X between 1258 and

Roofscape of La Mezquita.

1260. It has *azulejo* panels and lobed niches which spring from the floor in very sympathetic Mudéjar style. The floor level has risen and covers the bases of the columns, except where deliberately exposed, and so the present floor tells us nothing about the old. On the east exterior wall arcades and balconies were added to small upper rooms south of the *mihrab* including the Chapter House, Treasury and Sacristy. Despite additions and infirmities, La Mezquita is unique and cannot lose its claim to be the foremost Islamic monument in Spain.

The **Convento de Santa Clara** (*Calle del Rey Heredia*) retains its once Muslim towers and battlements and a staircase which turns on its own axis in the former minaret; this, square-cut and strong as a bastion, is probably 10th-century in date. The marble columns are probably Visigothic or earlier. A long and tranquil plaza accommodates this monument with grace. Because the convent doors are usually kept firmly closed, few people disturb the scene, reminiscent of the silent piazzas painted by de Chirico.

The **Capilla de San Bartolomé** (*Calle Salazar*) has fine stucco work, but the columns, from some Visigothic ruin, are the most striking feature.

San Juan (*Lope de Hoces*) has a finely proportioned minaret with a double-horseshoe window divided by a slim column surmounted by a spirited capital on each face.

San Miguel (*Plaza San Miguel*) has a horseshoe arch over the side door and a rose window *à la Mauresque*, an improbable combination.

San Pablo (*Calle de San Pablo*) was originally Romanesque and dates from 1241. The stucco work rivals that of the synagogue.

Santiago (*Calle Agustín Moreno*) conceals no trace of the earlier mosque except for the 10th-century minaret, built of good Roman ashlar.

The tower of San Juan which still retains its typical Muslim window.

The **Puente Romano** brings the traveller into Córdoba from the south. A sudden rise in the water level swept the superstructure away some time before the arrival of the Muslims, who repaired it in 720 with stones taken from the old town walls. Later the arches also had to be strengthened and now the roadway has been raised, as the sunken triumphal arch and the **Torre de la Calahorra** demonstrate. The bridge is 250 m (275 yd) in length and carried on 16 arches. The Umayyad emirs built the Torre de la Calahorra on the farther side to be the anchor of their defences and it was extended by Enrique II after the reconquest. Since 1978 Arab generosity has turned it into an Islamic Museum which houses two important recent models. That of the Alhambra is of interest because it shows the gardens within and without

The waterwheel on the bank of the Guadalquivir.

as they most probably were and disposes of their present misleading aspect. As important is the very large-scale model of La Mezquita showing it as it was before the reconquest, complete with 900 columns and its beam ceilings. Elsewhere there are models of Arab irrigation.

By the river are water meadows and mills, some on islets, mostly hidden by trees now that the water level has fallen. They, and all but one waterwheel, are ruined. The largest disappeared at the end of the 15th century, but it could not have compared with the great wheels of Syria.

The Visigothic walls were restored before 717 and doubled in extent. Apart from fragments a short stretch remains on the western side of the city, and there is another stretch, rebuilt after the reconquest, near the grandiose **Puerta del Almodóvar** between two typical Muslim towers. The fortifications have been heavily restored and the landscape of ordures which stank below them in medieval times has been replaced by municipal gardens. The old fortress was rebuilt by Alfonso XI in 1382 and dubbed the **Alcázar Nuevo**. The gardens beside the great pool are Renaissance with 19th- and 20th-century additions and the plants are ones that no Umayyad ever saw. Diagonally across the plaza, the baths of the emir's residence (subsequently the palace of the archbishop and now converted into an orphanage), have been excavated to roof level but are a mere token of what they were after brutal restoration. The Archbishop's Palace is the top layer of a four-decker sandwich of Roman, Visigoth and Islamic remains. Its patio is splendidly spacious. It is interesting that the building lies not parallel to but diagonally beside La Mezquita. The **Puerta de Sevilla**, which is certainly Umayyad, may prove to have been part of an aqueduct. The Avenida Victoria is the Champs Elysées of Córdoba, with gardens devoted to the muses but also with Mudéjar revival dovecotes. The spectacular example of this period of architecture is the colossal academy near the bus station off the Avenida de la República Argentina.

WALLS, GATES AND THE ALCÁZAR DE LOS REYES CRISTIANOS

The **Puerta del Almodóvar** leads into the **Barrio de la Judería** or Jewish quarter, which was once enclosed in its own wall. The **synagogue** was built by Simon Mejeb in 1315

THE JEWISH QUARTER AND BEYOND

and is an eminent example of Mudéjar decoration cut in smooth plaster, called decadent by some purists. Over all is a colonnade with windows at every second step, coupled colonnettes and seven-lobed arches. In the courtyard, a stone was the only memorial to Maimonides until recently. Now there is a life-size statue seated in an alley named after him. The oldest houses in this quarter appear to be those closest to the walls, to which they still have access, although it is no longer possible to walk to La Mezquita along them. Beneath them lurk Roman remains, including a barrel-vaulted cellar, one at least with a tessellated pavement in good condition. These homes still have long, shallow rooms besides patios and those ever-changing levels which make Islamic domestic architecture so full of visual surprises.

The rest of the old quarters around the mosque retain the atmosphere of a Muslim time poignantly, and if rebuilt houses are now taller they conform to the former sites, although present developments show increasingly little respect for the past. The **Casa de los Cea**, also called Casa del Indiano (House of the Indian) (*Plaza Angel de Torres*), Plateresque though its portal may be, suggests the luxury of these small mansions before the reconquest, as does patio after patio. They have been altered but they were altered throughout the five hundred years of Muslim rule. **La Casa de los Caballeros de Santiago** (House of the Knights of St James) (*Plaza de Valdelasgranas*) reveals greater Islamic influence with its lobed arches between coupled columns. The **Palacio del Marqués de Viana** (*Rejas Don Gome*) follows the form of a dream mansion with its 14 patios and houses an eclectic collection of minor works of art.

PALACIO JERÓNIMO PAEZ (The Provincial Archaeological Museum) (*Plaza de Jerónimo Paez*)

This building is a delight with its spacious courtyard and columned galleries, reminiscent of both Roman and Islamic times, although it was built in the 16th century. The display of mainly modest treasures dates back to Iberian times. Among the small collection of Islamic finds are braziers inscribed with Qu'ranic texts dating from 997. There is also the stag which surmounted the fountain at Madinat az-Zahra' and was given to 'Abd ar-Rahman III by the Emperor Constantine VII. It is symbolic of the goodwill that existed between emperor and caliph, and the enamelling has all the qualities of Byzantine craftsmanship.

Madinat az-Zahra' is slowly being reborn out of the mud and rubble of its three esplanades. The idyllic palatine city lies about 6 km (4 miles) west from Córdoba and is refreshed by breezes from the river below it. Plentiful and sweet water came down from springs which are now difficult of access in the foothills of the Sierra Morena. The city was begun by 'Abd ar-Rahman III in November 936 in order to escape the turmoil of his crowded capital and it was named after his most loved wife. Some of the work was carried out by his son, al-Hakam II. With its guards, gardeners, officials and womenfolk, the household amounted to some 20,000 people. For this reason it was not a garden suburb but a city. Some buildings probably reached four storeys in height like the extant Casa del Carbón at Granada. Only the royal plaisance and patios could have nurtured plants but the shade of orchards spread beyond the walls. At the lowest level, the formal parterres in front of the re-roofed pavilion of 'Abd ar-Rahman III, the **Salón Rico**, possessed four pools with a fine belvedere at their centre; it and the Salón were reflected in the pool between them. The Salón was the centre of ceremonial, hence the gorgeous decoration, which relates to that executed for the son of this remarkable caliph in La Mezquita. But here it is not executed in plaster but in stone. Paintwork and fabrics are lacking. The proximity of a *hammam* suggests that here was the centre of the caliph's personal life, such as it could be, but in fact the

MADINAT AZ-ZAHRA'

Madinat az-Zahra': a pool (now dry) in the gardens below the pavilion.

Madinat az-Zahra':
intricately carved tree
of life.

residential area was on the upper terrace. The caliph's apartments, the **Dar al-Mulk**, consisted of several rooms with modest patios hedging in an inner and an innermost section where there was a central hall with alcoves and modest chambers off it. These apartments were altered by al-Hakam II. The outer apartments have collapsed onto the middle terrace below. Beyond the walled gardens, reached across a bridge from the Salón Rico, is the mosque, with a porticoed court and with five aisles within.

Above the mosque, a file of 15 arches, four of which have been rebuilt, admitted to the **Dar al-Yund** (East Hall), the military area on the middle terrace which also included lodgings for officials. A ramp permitted horsemen to ride straight onto the parade ground. These intricate quarters centre on a cruciform basilical hall where triple-arched arcades, so much in the rhythm of Umayyad taste, open up the heart of these once lofty barracks. On the south, two houses for senior ministers flank a narrow street.

The palace is related to the lost country retreat of 'Abd ar-Rahman, founder of the dynasty in Spain, at Rusafa. The plan, which is stiff with the symbolism of majesty, relates to that of the desert palaces of Syria where the Umayyads were influenced by the villas of the Eastern Roman Empire, only to encounter those of the Western Empire when the dynasty approached its extinction. The use of the vegetal decoration to match the garden without; the lacelike carving of capitals in the manner of Constantinopolitan churches such as Sancta Sophia; flowers; every form of acanthus leaf; panel after panel; marble columns and terracotta or marble-tiled pavements — all make for an architectonic variety of form. This rare achievement confronted the Berber army of al-Mansur who, driven by those devastating impulses of jealousy that savage the human race, attacked and des-poiled it.

This paradise was put to sword and flame on 4 November 1010. The partially devastated site was visited by Almohad tourists and others who stole or purchased. Pedro I re-used material already plundered for another palace in Sevilla. The stones continued to be looted for buildings in Córdoba until 1408 when the monks of St Jerome built the Valparaiso monastery. Ricardo Velázquez carried out rescue opera-tions from 1911 until he died in 1923. More important work continued under Felix Hernández Giménez with plans

Madinat az-Zahra': heavily restored arcading in the former palace.

drawn up on a more scientific basis and with reconstruction beginning in 1944. The restoration advances rapidly but much remains to be done. Archaeologists toil in order to piece together impossible jigsaws, yet the elements do indeed fit and make sense even if one suspects some of them were made to conform. What is there is enough to set the imagination sparkling without excessive rebuilding, a solution that would have dubious justification.

BAENA (*Bayyana*)

This was a prosperous Muslim city with vineyards, gardens and olive groves, for the soil was rich and water plentiful. The solid fortress had an internal wall which was built first. It was taken by assault by Ferdinand III in 1240. In the upper town inside the Islamic walls is the square-domed Torre del Sol. The Mudéjar **Convento de la Madre de Dios** is relatively unmolested and possesses notable wooden ceilings.

BELMEZ

This was once a most formidable castle in a troubled region. There were additions and alterations after the reconquest. From afar it stands like a cone on the plateau but when close to it one sees that the rock has been bitten into to create a spectacular overhang which might have inspired Giorgione. A square keep rises rigidly out of the walls and its round towers.

Belmez: from its commanding position on a crag, the castle dominates the road to Badajoz and Portugal.

BUJALANCE

The Romans founded the castle which was rebuilt for 'Abd ar-Rahman III in 935 with seven towers. The ruins are impressive. It was the haunt of a legendary bagpiper who played for one peseta and stopped for ten.

CABRA

The Cabra of the audacious count who captured Boabdil of

Granada (see **Lucena**), it was important for its marble quarry 14 km (9 miles) to the north, which supplied the masons working on La Mezquita of Córdoba. The very early church of **San Domingo** rebuilt in the 16th century is a fascinating cake of jumbled bits and pieces of masonry, as if some overgrown child had been at play. For a change, a castle and not a church was concocted out of the mosque, which results in an unusual pattern of flowing stone and stilted arches. Both Roman and Visigoth have also left ghostly traces. Cabra was the birthplace in the ninth century of the much-loved blind minstrel, Mukaqqim, originator of the *zajal* stanza and precursor of the troubadours.

EL VACÁR
Castles as grand as this were also caravansarays or major staging posts between mere watch-towers positioned, in this case, every 10km (6 miles) or so along the river valley which the main highway follows. El Vacar was the first important stop on the way to Extremadura; today, even though in ruins and seemingly low-lying because of the extent of its walls, it is still a model of military exactitude, with a tower at each corner and one in the centre of each flanking wall. The modest entry is tucked in the lea of a corner tower.

LORA DEL RÍO
The Muslim castle is of early date and little altered except by time.

LUCENA
The Conde de Cabra anticipated the fall of Granada by capturing Boabdil, the last sultan, in 1483, nine years too soon. He held him to ransom in the octagonal tower which still stands. The town was chiefly inhabited by Jews until the bigoted Almohads expelled them. **San Mateo** has a fine timber ceiling.

SANTA MARÍA DE TRASSIERRA (Nr Madinat az-Zahra')
The former Almohad mosque, *c.*1200, was built within the walls of a fortress from which the surrounding area was kept in check. It was converted into a chapel. Beyond the town is a nine-arched Islamic bridge of great beauty.

GRANADA, ANDALUCÍA

Granada was a city populated by Jews when in 1012 the Berber Zirids retreated from Elvira to the safety of the heights of the Alhambra. They ruled briefly from the *Alcazaba* during the period of the Ta'ifa kings. The last Zirid ruler was 'Abdul Allah ibn Buluggin, the all-too intelligent chronicler of his times and a Machiavelli who failed from lack of ruthlessness. He was caught between Alfonso VI and the Christian north and Yusuf ibn Tashfin, leader of the fanatical Almoravid Berbers from the Maghrib, south across the water.

Out of the chaos of the petty kingdoms, Muhammad I came to rule over the city and province of Granada in 1231 and it is astonishing that this sultanate survived to be the last of the Islamic states in Spain, only to fall in 1492 after years of glory. The long survival of this state was due to the division among the Christian kingdoms, but it could not survive their united strength, symbolized by the marriage of Ferdinand and Isabella. That fact, and the shrinking of the Muslims' territory as they leased more and more land to Christians as grazing for their immense flocks of sheep — the supply of 600 head to the court by the Cistercians made no visible inroad on their flocks — meant that the little oasis of Muslim rule was doomed. Previously the Nasrids had paid tribute to Castile who found this preferable to conquest, because if there were an excess of sheep there were too few Christian subjects with whom to populate new territories. The Nasrids also maintained a cunning alliance with Aragón. Their greatest enemy was the Islamic Maghrib, out of which had come the puritanical Almoravids and Almohads. The Nasrids were lucky to contain such bands as did cross the Straits. Now, the court also had to face the fanaticism of the religious leaders, whose incitement of the humble people to hatred towards their future Christian masters was to prove suicidal. When the end came, it left a people unable to accommodate to change and who were partially themselves to blame for the hostility of the united Spain of the 16th century. Fortunately

(*Opposite*) Granada: the garden of the Generalife palace.

65

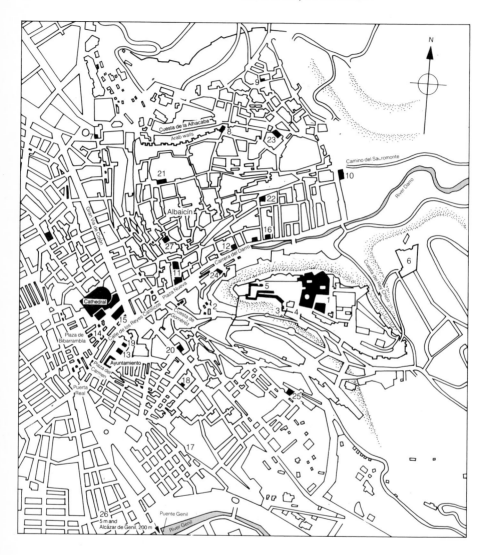

the more intelligent were quick to adapt: enduring families, who escaped the hunters of the Inquisition not least because their skills were essential to a civilized existence, adopted new Christian names and became part of the social structure of the realm. Many suffered and died or were expelled. These Moriscoes were not welcomed in North Africa, partly because of their numbers but also because they were a polyglot community divided among themselves and unable to establish any sort of unity in exile. To those who remained, whether genuine converts or sharp-witted pragmatists, Spanish architecture owes the Mudéjar style.

THE ALHAMBRA

The Alhambra was not one building, but a whole range, which took refuge behind magnificent defences on a mountain spur overlooking the city. Its palaces occupied large areas of which some are now gardens where gladioli and other plants unknown to Muslims bloom. The rulers were surrounded by the populace, of whom there were enough to warrant a great mosque, and lived in the midst of government offices and the barracks of their unruly soldiery. They liked to escape to the peace of the **Generalife** and other country estates where the hunting was good and mobs were unknown.

The heavenly gardens and the sky are idealized in the palace decoration, vast amounts of which today are copied from moulds, including the fine calligraphic friezes. These are mainly in Nakhsi script, but there are examples of floral ancient Kufic. The original paint has either faded or been restored, and the fabled furnishings are gone, save for one vase (the *Jarrón de la Alhambra*) in the Museum. Even Owen Jones, the most influential 19th-century authority on ornament, could not recapture the original kaleidoscope of colour, yet the repaired vase gives an idea of what must have been, as do silks in various museums, for example the few but pristine lengths in the Lázaro Galdiano Institute in Madrid.

Out of the Plaza Nueva the Cuesta de Gomérez winds up to the **Puerta de las Granadas** (Gate of the Pomegranates), three of which ride on top of this grand entry. Hidden in the wooded hillside is the **Puerta de Bibarrambla** (Sand Gate), which once stood in the middle of the town but was stranded here when the modern city developed at the foot of the hill. The path leads up past the fountain of Charles V to the **Puerta de Justicia**, dating from 1348-9. It was built by Yusuf I and has a double bent entry turned back on itself through two lofty halls. The massive tower enfolds a magnificent horseshoe arch under deep brick eaves. Behind is a smaller arch which retains the original doors and their fine furniture. Above is Yusuf's inscription and cut out of an Islamic tiled tympanum is a niche in which Ferdinand and

(*Opposite*) Granada
1. Alhambra;
2. Puerta de las Granadas; 3. Puerta de Justicia; 4. Puerta del Vino;
5. Alcazaba;
6. Generalife;
7. Puerta de Elvira;
8. Puerta Nueva;
9. Casa de los Mascarones;
10. Casa Chapiz;
11. Casa de los Pisas;
12. *hammam*;
13. Casa del Carbón;
14. Alcaicería;
15. Casa del Cabildo Antiguo; 16. Casa de Castril; 17. Cuarto Real; 18. Casa de los Girones; 19. Casa de los Duques de Abrantes; 20. Casa de los Tiros;
21. Convento de Santa Isabel; 22. San Juan de los Reyes;
23. San Salvador;
24. Santa Ana;
25. San Cecilio;
26. San Sebastián;
27. San José.

The Alhambra
1. Puerta del Vino;
2. Tourist entrance;
3. Mexuar;
4. Oratory;
5. Cuarto Dorado;
6. Patio de los
Arrayanes; 7. Sala de
la Barca; 8. Salón del
Trono; 9. Patio de los
Leones; 10. Sala de
los Abencerrajes;
11. Sala de los Reyes;
12. Sala de las Dos
Hermanas; 13. Sala
de los Ajimeces;
14. *hammam*;
15. Palacio del
Partal.

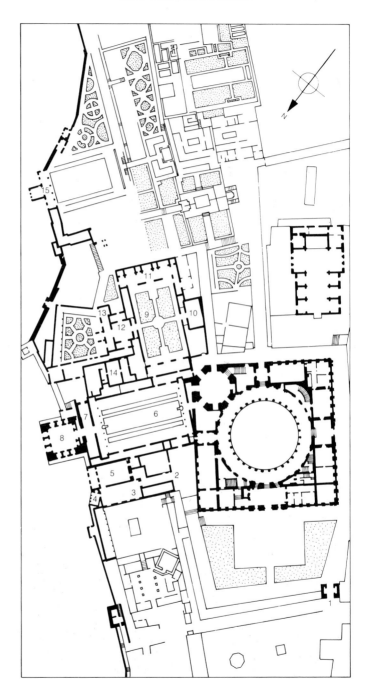

The Alhambra seen from the Albaicín.

Isabella placed a Virgin, in somewhat suburban taste. The road climbs to the brick and stucco **Puerta del Vino** (Wine Gate), which was the entrance to the urban area, with benches for the watch on either side under the tunnel vault supporting the upper guardroom. It was built by Muhammad II but altered later. The east façade has a fine pair of windows between stucco reliefs under deep eaves formed of the usual layer of bricks; like the Gate of Justice, the spandrels of the horseshoe arch carry false voussoirs but are enriched by lattice reliefs round the discs to the sun and moon. This façade is the later, dating from the reign of Muhammad V in the 14th century. That on the western side is of plain stone with no ornament other than the curious

(*Above*) The Jarrón de la Alhambra.

(*Left*) The Alcazaba seen from the Alhambra.

grille of voussoirs between small windows. Austerity gives the gate strength in spite of repairs made with slim bricks like slices of toast, typical of Mudéjar architecture.

Their kinsman, the Vezir Nagrella, had it brought up to date as a fortress into which the townsfolk could retreat when Berber raiders attacked. The works were carried out by the Almoravids and Almohads before the Zirid clan took Granada. Thus it was in the 12th century that the **Alcazaba** took its present form with the addition of formidable towers within curtain walls. Three towers look inwards over the later palaces: the **Torre del Adarguero** on the east, the **Torre Quebrada** in the centre — a stolid bulwark which may be the earliest — and the **Torre del Homenaje** (Tower of Homage, or Keep) on the west. In it the emir first had his apartments with one hall under a dome which is supported by reversed squinches like pouter-pigeons at the corners of the octagon. The stalwart **Torre de la Pólvora** (Gunpowder Tower) has stairs up to the sentry walks and the varying levels round the **Torre de la Vela**, the grand watch-tower and barrack that crouches like Despair on top of the prison. The gardens in this area have nothing to do with the military realities of the Muslim period, while the huge rampart over the southern snout of the hill was added after the reconquest when the urban gate was destroyed. Muhammad had erected a powerful postern, unusual in Islamic fortress architecture, on the west flank with the usual bent entrance. This gave access to and from the town, which at that time covered the steep slopes wherever it could cling.

Within the lower walls like gums awaiting false teeth is a grid of excavations at hip- and knee-level which include a vast cistern and barrack rooms. Here **La Puerta de las Armas** is inserted into brick walls and has brick voussoirs clamped by the triple teeth of the horseshoe arch and its frame, nicely looped at the apex. The *Alcazaba* was formidable even after the introduction of gunpowder but today it is a vantage point from which to look down on the later buildings and trace their forms, including the bite taken out of them by the palace of Charles V. One sees that each element is independent, which was partly due to the tradition that a son inherited his father's clothes but not his house, and so through lack of space would eventually add on a pavilion.

To visit the Alhambra in chronological order one would

have to be able to fly to and fro like a bird; even then, demolitions and Renaissance-style gardens would frustrate one's attempt. It is wise therefore to follow the route recommended in the scholarly guide by the Director of the Museum of the Alhambra, Professor Don Antonio Fernández-Puertas.

The way in is modest and lies in shadows, because Islamic palaces were introverted and without the pomp of Western façades. On passing through the back door, so to speak, the

The façade of the Comares palace across the Cuarto Dorado.

(*Opposite*) The Patio de los Arrayanes in the Palace of Comares dating from 1370.

visitor begins in the **Mexuar** (*al-Mashwar*, or Hall of Audience) of the **Palacio de Comares**, which takes its dimensions from the rebuilding by Muhammad V in 1365. It has a pretty gallery and four columns that formerly supported the lantern which in Islamic days let in the Eye of God. Considerable alterations include the bringing of decoration from other rooms. At the end is the Oratory which had its floor lowered in deference to western habits of standing where a Muslim would have sat cross-legged in order to look out of the casements. These are as open as an arcade. A second row of windows with elegant plaster lattices runs above, the one row for light and the other for air. The chamber is virginal in its whiteness and the polygonal *mihrab* niche exquisitely adorned. The timber ceiling is flat, while the present door was cut for tourists. Significantly, since the oratory may predate the Mexuar, the original entry led to the *Alcazaba* and the Emir's apartments. The *soigné* hedges of the garden are not Muslim.

The Mexuar leads into a handsome patio with a shallow pool which takes its name from the redecorated **Cuarto Dorado** built in the Mudéjar style after the reconquest. Across this court is the notable but restrained façade of the Palace of Comares dating from 1370. The expansive eaves were to protect Muhammad V when he received visitors, for on the left is the door to the royal apartments while on the right is that used by the administrative officers who were kept strictly apart. The two rectangular doors have double windows above for the ladies of the court with small linked windows between; the whole is so beautifully balanced in its proportions that even the slight rise in the pavement level is disturbing because decorations were subordinate to exacting mathematics, the culmination of training and experience.

Detail of doorway between the Patio de los Arrayanes and the Patio de los Leones.

From this court the royal door admits to a handsome hall and stair by way of the bent entrance to the **Patio de los Arrayanes**. Here two shallow fountains splash lazily to fill the rectangular pool between low hedges of myrtles which give their name to this inner garden. The pool cools the lofty halls which flank it, reflects light into their shade and doubles the arcades of this paradise by reflection, a reflection in which to study the stars. There are seven-arched arcades with panels of woven decoration, the centre arch always taller to reveal no plain horseshoe but one which, under its triple windows, hints at the *muqarnas* or stalactite exuberan-

ces to come. On either side of the lean court are the four sets of chambers for the wives with the windows of their winter galleries above. These long rooms have deep divan alcoves but little decoration survives. The hall at the south end was destroyed by the Palace of Charles V but the latticed gallery remains. Here were the apartments of the princes and their tutors. At the opposite end was the **Sala de la Barca**, which was the private chamber of the sultan by night as well as by day, for it too has alcoves for divans at either end. Over each alcove rises a star-shot semi-dome to ensure sweet dreams for the sovereign, while the long chamber between was roofed with another deep ceiling shaped like a boat. The decoration includes fine inscriptions forming verses of an epic poem above the *azulejos*, panels of star formation tiles in green, white and black, mauve and buff. These were all part of the refitting of the palace between 1362 and 1370 by Muhammad V when the rich plaster ornament was completed. Between the salon and the throne-room is a corridor

The Salón del Trono.

leading to the private oratory hardly bigger than a *mihrab* where the prince could lead himself in prayer; at the other end is a stairway up to his winter quarters. The major room in this palace is the **Salón del Trono** (throne-room), which was built for Yusuf I before 1354. The presence of the ruler, who would be seated mysteriously before the light of the central window hung about with pure white silk, was the climax of the approach of ambassador or subject. The room is an amazing achievement. Its massive walls create lesser rooms within recessed windows which have pairs of lights above them. Today the vast shallow plaster wall between these windows and the star-latticed arcade below the roof is uncoloured, although the ruffled surface, tinged red by brickdust in places, glows in the soft sunlight. In Islamic days, though, it was as colourful as a tapestry might have been had man been able to weave one so immense. Into the vegetal or geometric designs are set panels of quotations from the Qu'ran as well as lyric verses to human happiness. The workmanship of the *azulejo* dado is as fine as all the rest. The ceiling is a masterpiece of carpentry too intricate to imitate. In three dimensions is traced the journey of the seven heavens among the stars of paradise at the crown of the dome where is the ultimate heaven, the seat of God.

Inscription on the wall of the wives' apartments in the Patio de los Arrayanes.

Muhammad V wished to differentiate between the seat of sovereignty and his personal quarters and so built the most famous court, the **Patio de los Leones** (Lion Court), at right-angles to the Court of the Myrtles. This was reached through the **Sala de los Mozarabes**, deprived of its much-extolled ceiling by an explosion. The hall opens out to form a pavilion of arcades and slender columns along stalactite arches and domes. This faces its counterpart along the main axis of a watercourse fed by two miniature waterspouts either side of a crossing where stands the polygonal basin of the period of Muhammad V above the backs of the marble lions. These gruff fellows were made for the sultan and were not brought from the palace of Samuel ibn Nagrella, the great Jewish vezir, as was once supposed. For a long time this fountain was disfigured by a baroque centrepiece and was hoisted incongruously on a central pier. On the south side the water trickles out of the **Sala de los Abencerrajes** with its central fountain under an immense *muqarnas* dome with stars and cupolas abounding but no longer brilliantly painted, although traces of colour remain. Even so, the effect is of an

unmatched firework where each element descends out of the other. Here legend says that Muhammad IX saw the head of the Abencerrajes clan decapitated for treason and here, symbolically, his own blood was washed away when his throat was cut by a usurper. The less macabre truth is that the hall was reserved for winter festivals: summer entertainment took place in the **Sala de los Reyes** (Hall of the Kings) at the far end of the court. This long chamber is traditional and yet a strange shape, in which a series of recessed compartments suggest *loges* for guests, although, as with most boxes, they would have had a poor view of the performers. Three larger recesses are flanked by smaller ones which could have been pantries for the servitors or for courtiers. Three rooms retain their painted ceilings. They tell tales of chivalry including that of a noble Muslim winning the heart of a maiden from her Christian lover. It is a room which appears both open and shut where alternating areas of light contrast with those of darkness. There are vistas beyond its arcades which are the life-blood of the Alhambra and other great Islamic buildings, corresponding to the more pedestrian *chambres de parade* of Western palaces. The abode of bliss, this inner place, would be a marvel to visit by moonlight and utterly overwhelming were lamps lit inside and out. For the patio flows into the arcades and reaches each recess until inside or out loses all meaning.

On the remaining side of the patio is the **Sala de las Dos Hermanas** (Hall of the Two Sisters) with upper winter

(*Opposite*) The Patio de los Leones is pillared like an open hall.

(*Above*) A detail of a capital and a console.

(*Left*) One of the painted ceilings of the Sala de los Reyes.

The sunburst that is the dome of the Sala de las Dos Hermanas.

quarters. The sisters are not hidden beauties but, more prosaically, two large marble slabs. This magnificent hall is banded with fine verses written to order by the vezir Ibn Zamrak in honour of the circumcision of Muhammad V's son. The dome is a shooting star that has exploded and then frozen in space: *muqarnas* domes like crystals could evolve no farther. Here, too, light and vista are interspersed with sudden views through casements across the city to the mountains or to some intimate court with a single tree. Architecture has reached its Everest and leaves no other height for the Nasrid style to climb. The long slim **Sala de los Ajimeces** has bare walls except for double-arched windows above which is a fine *muqarnas* ceiling. The central arch opens into the Mirador or gazebo of Lindaraja looking down onto a garden where a pool formerly reflected the projecting room. The rooms off this apartment, including the remodelled Peinador de la Reina, belong to the period after the reconquest, as does the present Lindaraja garden below. Off this is the entrance to the Comares *hammam*, or Arab bath, which has been altered and restored. Charles V made use of it and had the marble floors laid.

The **Palacio del Partal** dates from the beginning of the 14th century and is the oldest part of the palace although the last to be visited. It is now a simple pavilion, the far wall almost as open as the terrace facing the large pool. The balance of the design has been distorted by the use of marble columns to support the five arches of the portico, in place of the original piers, in order to match those of the inside wall. The tower has fine workmanship, although in poor condition, but the basin has been enhanced by two large dribbling lions once believed to have come from the Maristan, the city hospital, wantonly destroyed in the 1840s. The oratory set in a corner was built for Yusuf I before 1354 and it is captivating in its details, as is its fine *mihrab* niche with its horseshoe doorway. The building is so modest that it might be a sentry-box for a king to play at soldiers. The garden layout is not Islamic nor are the species of flowers authentic. Some idea of the actual grounds in Muslim times can be obtained from the charming model in the Torre de la Calahorra in Córdoba. The present gardens extend over the foundations of a palace of Yusuf III dating from the early 15th century. The walls and towers are much restored. The **Torre de los Picos**, or machicoulis, was enlarged by

A detail of *muqarnas* work.

Muhammad III and the interior altered by Ferdinand and Isabella. That of the Qadi, or magistrate, is a watch-tower but the **Torre de la Cautiva** (Imprisoned Lady) is a miniature palace built by Yusuf I. On entering by the bent entrance, one is taken by surprise, for room has been found for an inner court. The windows and the decoration are sensitive but the dome has been restored. Poems run along the walls. The next tower, the **Torre de las Infantas** (of the Princesses) is inferior and dates from c. 1400 and the reign of Muhammad VII. The north-west range of walls is rarely explored and is of little interest apart from the lofty **Puerta de Siete Suelos** (Gate of Seven Storeys), which has been respectably restored. In 1971 a bridge across the ravine was built to unite the gardens of the Alhambra to those of the Generalife, giving the mistaken impression that the country estate was an extension of the palaces. It was but one of several rural retreats and was reached only after a rough ride. Muhammad V was stranded helplessly when a palace revolution occurred while he was week-ending there. A loyal groom brought him a mount and he escaped to Guadix and eventually regained his throne.

This palace suffered first from Bourbon neglect and then at the hands of a minor nobleman without the money to keep it up. After a fire in 1958, the form of the lost apartments was at last understood. The present gardens make a nonsense of the place, for it was a working farm with extensive orchards, vegetable gardens and pastures for flocks and herds. A visitor dismounted at the lower patio and climbed the stairs to the long, rectangular garden court, the **Patio de la Acequia** (watercourses) which stretched out in front of the palace. This garden was divided into lean, shallow basins and had a belvedere looking down towards the Alhambra, so near and yet so far. The arcading at the north end of the garden is original. A long hall was the royal apartment and a distinctive tower may have contained the throne. The retiring room above is much altered. Some of this work was due to the restorations of Ismail I in 1319. Stairs lead up from the hall to the **Patio del Ciprés de la Sultana** (Court of the Queen's Cypress), remodelled in Renaissance times. A water stair brings a splash of the Villa d'Este to Spain, while the belvedere at the top is Nasrid.

The support walls of the Generalife survive in part, especially below the lower terraces towards the Alhambra, and their style suggests that the estate was an early possession of the Nasrid dynasty.

CITY WALLS
AND GATES

The high 11th-century walls were built by the Zirids and stretch from the **Puerta Nueva** (New Gate), also called Arco de las Pesas (Arch of the Weights), to the **Puerta de Elvira** with its horseshoe arch. The Puerta Nueva with its bent entrance had the added refinement of a slope, now a stairway. There are also traces of the Puerta Hizna Román near the Plaza Larga. The Nasrids extended the walls to encompass the Albaicín and added square towers but much of this was demolished when the city was modernized, although the **Puerta de Fajalauza** survives. The wall on each side of the River Darro ends in towers between which was the wooden sluice gate known as the **Puente de los Tableros**. Beyond this point the walls extend to the summit of the Alhambra plateau to end anchored to two small forts. South of the city is the **Puente Genil**, tenth-century but frequently rebuilt. Near it, Ferdinand and Isabella saw the Christian flag raised to signal the surrender of the Alhambra.

STREETS AND
QUARTERS

The most important quarter is the **Albaicín**, which can be viewed from the Alhambra. Its Islamic past is recognizable in its warren of tight whitewashed streets working their way to and fro across the hillside and in the shady gardens of the grander mansions. The Albaicín (*Ribad al-Bayyazin*) takes its name from the Company of the Falconers. From here, the views of the Alhambra are just as spectacular as those from it. Numerous houses and lanes are little altered. Actual houses remain intact, as can be seen in Calle Santa María, for example, or the Calle del Perdón, especially No. 32, or Calle del Agua, No. 37. The former is unmolested in its simplicity while the latter is the **Casa de los Mascarones** (Masks), which was remodelled in the 19th century when the masks were first displayed upon its façade. Especially in the humbler quarters, here an adobe and there a timber-frame house sustain Islamic building traditions although dateless in themselves. On the ascent to the Monastery of San Miguel, the Camino del Sacromonte, other examples include the

The austere patio of the Casa del Carbón, once a hostel for merchants.

Casa de Chapiz. This residence of a convert to Christianity has a Mudéjar patio and is now the School of Arabic Studies. Down by the river are the **Casa de los Pisas**, where the mystic San Juan de la Cruz died, in the Plaza Santa Ana, and the **Casa de los Moriscos** off the Plaza Albaida. The quarter hides much of the past but has yielded fine timber ceilings which will be conserved.

The **Hammam** (*Bañuelo*) (*Carrera del Darro*) is the only Moorish bath in the city open to the public apart from the grander example of the Alhambra, although others survive. The **Casa del Carbón** (*Funduq al-Yadida*), briefly a coal exchange, is the only remaining merchants' lodging and exchange. It is built round a square court beyond a high and strong door under projecting brick eaves. The horseshoe entry opens into a small vestibule with a second smaller gate under twin windows. The once lavish decoration has withered, including the later ducal arms, but a fine inscription remains. There is nothing monumental inside. Brick piers support two galleries which extend round all four sides. There are 60 cells.

The **Alcaicería** (*Plaza de Bibarrambla*) is a conclave of narrow streets rebuilt in the 19th century aping the former Islamic silk market which once flourished on this site. Horseshoe arches do their best but shop windows scarcely recall the past.

The **Casa del Cabildo Antiguo** (Old Council House),

PUBLIC BUILDINGS

The resplendent gateway to the Casa del Carbón.

beside the Cathedral, has retrieved its original name of Palacio de la Madiraza or Madrasa, for it was the principal college of the Muslim university built in 1348/9. The shape of the court and one domed octagonal mosque is little altered but the rest is changed completely. The former Council Hall has a fine wooden ceiling.

The **Museo Nacional de Arte Hispano-Musulman** is presently in the Palace of Charles V in the Alhambra but will soon move to a new building in the woods above the Alhambra. There is an exceptionally choice collection of ceramics and much else, including an ivory plaque and rare fabrics of the Nasrid period, which form a unique collection. The **Casa de Castril** (*43 Carrera del Darro*) dates from *c.* 1539 and has some Islamic exhibits in its collection.

PALACES

The **Cuarto Real**, or former Monastery of San Domingo (*Campillo Alto*) replaces the orchard of a Nasrid royal palace. The lofty hall possesses a dado of *azulejos* and elaborate plasterwork. Above are recent double horseshoe arches over 20 windows with plaster lattices. The ceiling could be contemporaneous with the original palace.

The **Casa de los Girones** (*Calle San Domingo*) has partial remains of an important residence which had a long patio closed by a portico on its west side. In the arcaded halls and some smaller rooms the plasterwork was moulded over a coloured ground and could date from the 13th century. Several Arabic inscriptions survive.

The **Alcázar Genil** (*Paseo del Violón* — Passage of the Double Bass) has been heavily restored at ground level but the upper part is magnificent. The tower room has 14th-century plasterwork.

The **Casa de los Duques de Abrantes** (*Plaza de Tovar*) is next door to the Casa del Carbón and its façade is Mudéjar Gothic.

The **Casa de los Tiros** (Palace of the Muskets) (*Plaza de los Tiros*) was built into the city wall and is a museum as well as the tourist office.

CHURCHES

The **Convento de Santa Isabel** (*Calle del Ladrón del Agua* — Street of the Water Thief), was the *Dar al-Horra* or Dower House of the Alhambra. Some walls survive, as do three arches in the patio at ground level below the gallery where

there are niches. The church has a notable wooden ceiling.
San Cecilio lies beneath the Hotel Alhambra, itself a
splendid mock-up of the 19th-century vision of a Nasrid
palace. The church is a hotchpotch with a tower vulgarly
restored in polychrome brick.
San José (*Plaza de San José*) is a church which may be built
on the foundations of a mosque; some tenth-century footings
survive. A complete horseshoe arch is encased in the south
wall. The bell-tower rises from the base of the minaret. Inside
are Mudéjar ceilings and a dome.
San Juan de los Reyes (*Calle de San Juan de los Reyes*) was
the first Catholic church built in Granada. The 11th- or 12-
century minaret is now the bell-tower.
San Salvador (*Plaza de San Salvador*) is the principal
church of the Albaicín, possibly built on the site of a tenth-
century mosque. The court of ablutions is discernible and the
cisterns have been preserved. Original brick interlace patterns still ornament the bell-tower. The *madrasa* or college is
lost but the inscription on a marble plaque once set in its
façade is now in the museum.
San Sebastián (*Paseo del Violón*) was a *rabita* or hermitage and is indeed the only one which survives in Spain. It
forms a modest square under an umbrella dome made up of
16 ribs supported on squinches. In these simple surround-
ings, Ferdinand and Isabella said farewell to Boabdil when
he left his Alhambra home for ever.
Santa Ana (*Plaza de Santa Ana*) is a Mudéjar church with
azulejos. The tower is lightened as it ascends by the
increased size of the apertures, in the manner of Byzantine
belfries in Ravenna and elsewhere. The finial of the minaret
is in the Alhambra Museum.

ALMUÑÉCAR
The ruined **Castillo de San Miguel** is of Islamic origin.
Originally the *Alcazaba* of the Muslims, it was completely
restored by Charles V. Salobrena, 15 km (9 miles) away is an
outpost of this defence system.

ATARFE
The ruins of Elvira have revealed traces of the Islamic as well
as the Roman city. Elvira and Jaén were the strongholds of
the Zirid emirs when the Caliphate disintegrated.

OTHER SITES
NEAR
GRANADA

BAZA (*Bastah*)

The town prospered under Islamic rule. Al-Idrisi, the geographer, wrote that it was rich with mulberry groves and a centre of the silk industry in the province. It was famous for its brocaded silk prayer rugs. There were olive groves and orchards in abundance while the mountains nearby produced *kohl* or galena (sulphide of antimony), used as eyeshadow and indispensable to the ladies of the Arab world to the present day. The population included many Mozarabs. The fortress is now a ruin.

ELVIRA (*see* ATARFE)

GUADIX (*Wadi As*)

The **Alcazaba** was begun in the ninth century but altered in the fifteenth. It is encircled by walls and towers. The Muslims moved the town the better to defend it. The silver mine is dead but not the swarms of young inhabitants in this town. Here cave dwellers have burrowed from time immemorial yet are not true troglodytes, for many have houses as well. It was an early Visigothic see of a metropolitan or bishop. Mulberry trees by the river testify to its silk production. It was to Guadix that Muhammad V fled when there was a revolt at the Alhambra.

LANJARÓN

This is a long white village in the midst of peaches, oranges, figs and pomegranates which also possesses mineral springs and a *hammam*. The now ruined castle held out after the fall of Granada but in 1500 was pounded by the artillery of Ferdinand of Aragón. The starving garrison surrendered but the black commander, overcome by the disgrace, if disgrace it were, flung himself from what remained of a tower. Ferdinand proceeded to shatter the columns of the mosque.

LAS ALPUJARRAS

This corner of the province of Granada was given to Boabdil and his followers as a refuge in 1492 but their life of modest hunting was ended in 1499. Boabdil left for humiliation in Africa. The descendants of his followers who chose to stay were driven to revolt in 1570 but the futile uprising was put down by Don Juan of Austria, the bastard son of Charles V, who was to defeat the Ottoman fleet at Lepanto. The survivors were uprooted and dispersed throughout Spain.

ALMERÍA, ANDALUCÍA

The **Alcazaba** of Almería was built on the order of 'Abd ar-Rahman III in the tenth century and enlarged in the eleventh. Its massive walls and towers twisting over every knuckle of the terrain descend from the crest of the hill in measured pace to where the whitewashed town was scattered like a fistful of sugar cubes until tourism crushed the suburbs under

Almería, Alcazaba: the fortifications are among the grandest in Spain.

masonry. The keep was added by Ferdinand of Aragón. The **Chapel of San Juan** began as a Mozarabic church but was converted into a mosque. The Almohads redecorated the *mihrab*. The cathedral was built in 1524 on the site of the Great Mosque. For 50 years during the 11th century Almería was a little emirate, but its fame must now rest on the splendid double horseshoe arch within an arch of the fortress. It was once a famous or infamous pirate stronghold until taken by Ferdinand, when the patriots sailed their ships across the water to, in a sense, reverse the charges.

OTHER SITES
NEAR ALMERÍA

ADRA
The Phoenicians inherited the perfect site for their port of Abdera, and the town prospered because of the quality of the fish, which was salted down for the winter. Some Islamic fortifications still stand, including two massive towers which are part of the line of castles and towers along the coast built mainly against pirates who included cousins of the Berber townsfolk. 23 km (14 miles) away **La Rábita** commemorates the fortified monastery of the dervishes who, though mystics, were nonetheless fierce fighters in defending the frontier. In this they were kin to the Christian military orders of chivalry which abounded in Spain.

BERJA
The town is famed for its lead mines. It has Muslim reservoirs which give an idea of the extensive engineering work carried out by the Arabs in order to irrigate their valleys and plains. The fortifications are tumbledown — an array of pillaged stone.

CASTELL DE FERRO
The castle is the remains of a defence post dependent on the castle at Almuñécar.

MOJÁCAR
Modernity has overwhelmed the white hilltop village, where until 20 years ago, veiled women still trampled their washing at the *fuente* in the old Moroccan manner. Then it was the most Islamic haunt in Spain where fingers were forked against the evil eye. But now the infernal visitor is the tourist.

CÁDIZ, ANDALUCÍA

Cádiz (*Jazirat Cadiz*), said to have been founded by Phoenicians in 1500 BC, may or may not be the oldest town in the west. Julius Caesar pompously called the place Urbs Julia Augusta Gaditana. The Visigoths followed but when the Muslims took it in 711 they regarded it as of little importance. The Vikings took it in 844 and 859 but their raids were never intended to consolidate a bridgehead. Finally, Alfonso the Wise captured it on 24 September 1262. It was the Pillars of Hercules and not Cádiz that excited medieval imaginations. The centre of the cult was a tower built by the Romans and demolished in 1145 by the then governor out of idiocy, believing a legend that treasure was buried in the foundations. This **'Ali** was a member of the powerful Maymum family whose claim to fame would be a cloud of dust. 'Ali had the masons remove the stones at ground level and replace them with wooden beams until the building rested on wood. Not only was this structure insecure but it caught fire. The tower crashed with a roar and a cloud of dust rose which was to keep housewives busy for days. The only treasure was the lead which bound the stones. Sensibly, the Almoravid emir had the numbskull assassinated — quietly, to avoid arousing the Maymum clan to arms.

ALGECIRAS (*El Gezira* or *al-Jazira al-Khaura*)
Despite its exciting history, or because of it, little that is Islamic remains except for fragments of an aqueduct. The Muslim town took its name from the Isla Verde, the Green Island, which lies like a natural mole in front of the town. The normal Islamic route to Africa was from here to Ceuta, 28 km (18 miles) away, but the practical Almohads cut the distance to 19 km (12 miles) by moving the embarkation point to Alcázarseguir. Algeciras was built on the hillside and protected by an arc of walls which reached the sea on either side. It was important enough to possess a fine *Alcazaba*. The Wadi an-Nahl (Honey Brook), which cut the town in two was often dry, but it fertilized the gardens and orchards on

either bank. The town was attacked by a Viking raiding party in 859 and the Mosque of the Banners next to the Sea Gate was burnt to the ground. 'Abd ar-Rahman built an arsenal in which to shelter his fleet but this was ruined in a raid by Berbers in 1011. The walls were not properly repaired until Yusuf ibn-Tashfin restored them in 1086. In 1173 the town was again laid waste by an army from Castile and was blockaded by Alfonso the Wise in 1278. The attack petered out and the Marinid Emir built a last palace in the country which reminded him of his residence in Fez and died there in 1286. Alfonso XI took the town after a long siege in 1344 but there was to be no peace yet, for the Sultan of Granada recaptured the town, only to destroy it in 1368–9.

ARCOS DE LA FRONTERA (*Madinat Arkush*)

The castle was considered impregnable but the Muslims were dislodged in 1264. The church of **San Pedro** rose like a phoenix from the ruins, which suggests that the struggle must have been ferocious, else the castle would have been repaired. Its strength was its position on the edge of an escarpment above the Rio Guadalete. Here and there in the vicinity traces of Islamic workmanship remain. Both the **Palacio de Águila** with its Mudéjar entrance and the **Ayuntamiento** (Town Hall) with fine ceilings have outstanding views. There are traces of a Visigothic past in **Santa**

Arcos de la Frontera, impregnable on its high cliffs.

María de la Asunción. The town is famous for its kestrels, which, like its stacked narrow streets, preserve a vividly medieval atmosphere.

BORNOS
The early Muslim fortress is remarkable for its deep cisterns.

CASTELLAR DE LA FRONTERA
The village was built within the walls of the 12th-century castle. It was to withstand a siege of long duration at the time of the reconquest.

EL PUERTO DE SANTA MARÍA
The town was built at the mouth of the Río Guadalete and from the 13th century was protected by the **Castillo de San Marcos** which has been extensively altered. The mosque remains recognizable and its *mihrab* intact, while a Mozarabic chapel is set in an enchanted courtyard.

JEREZ DE LA FRONTERA
After a fierce battle beside the Río Guadalete, in which the Visigoth Rodrigo met his ruin, the town was taken by the Arabs in 711 and became one of their fortified bases. The town was without a history until taken by Alfonso X in 1264.

The late 17th- to 18th-century church of **San Salvador** is built on the site of the main mosque, which had been of considerable size. The bell-tower of this collegiate church is in the Mudéjar style with Gothic elements, and its independence suggests that it predates the church. It stands upon a square base which is plain for half its height; with the addition of single large windows higher up its austerity wanes and the top storey is neatly capped. **San Dionisio** was built by Alfonso X but altered inside. Externally it is more Muslim than Gothic. It, too, has an austere bell-tower, the Torre de la Atalaya, enlivened by small windows, now blocked up. There is a patio overlooked by elegant Islamic paired windows divided by a small column with lobed voussoirs. There is interlacing brickwork on the flank of the church. The Mudéjar tower of the church of **San Miguel** is blue with *azulejos*, as is the late 17th-century façade. Other churches — **San Marcos, San Juan** and **San Lucas** — all have Mudéjar details. The most important Islamic monument is the **Alcázar** but it is not always open. Ruins and restoration are puzzling but foundations and footings indicate an early date. The octagonal tower is 12th-century, and a *hammam* in the keep was rebuilt after the reconquest.

Off the Sevilla road is the formidable **Torre de Melgorejo** which is part of a ruined castle incorporated into a farm.

JIMENA DE LA FRONTERA

This Muslim village and stronghold was not taken until 1431 because of its impregnable hilltop position. The defences grew out of the rock on three sides; a gateway evolves into three horseshoe arches. At one end of the ridge is a later keep but at the other is the present cemetery. The custom of protecting one's ancestors could have pagan roots: Roman tombstones were used in the construction of the fortress. The town was well-equipped to withstand a siege for the castle has its own spring and deep, vaulted cisterns. There are also cellars with barrel-vaulted ceilings for storage. The white town is crowded between a cliff and a precipitous slope.

MEDINA SIDONIA

The town gave its name to the dukedom of the commander of the Armada, from the notable Guzman family of grandees. The fortress is typical but subdued and there are sparse remains of Islamic walls but one fine horseshoe arch, the **Arco de la Pastora** (of the Shepherdess).

SAN FERNANDO

The promontory known as the Isla del León is overwhelmed by naval establishments. The **Romaldo Fortress** was built *c.* 1325 for Alfonso IX by Muslim architects and the result is an archetypal Almohad monument, with its sharp play of light and shade from square towers upholding rectangular walls.

SANLÚCAR DE BARRAMEDA

The town is near the battlefield where Rodrigo was vanquished by Tariq in 711 and it was not reconquered until 1264. The early castle retains one tower and a horseshoe arch but it is otherwise in ruins; two gates are all that remain of the considerable walls. Columbus sailed from here on his third voyage to America and Magellan on his voyage round the world. The church of **Nuestra Señora de la 'O'**, or Santa María, has a Mudéjar doorway with a carpet-weave of decoration above it as well as shields and their supporters.

JAÉN, ANDALUCÍA

The site is impregnable and even fights off the modern town. Jaén (*Jayyan*) was an important stage on the road north to Madrid but it is not clear where the caravans lodged if not in the **Castillo de Santa Catalina**, which was a remarkable fortress until altered after the reconquest. Now it is a Parador. A meagre stretch of town walls between towers is still standing. The lanes of the inner city, white houses and Mudéjar bell-towers help preserve the Muslim atmosphere. The cathedral replaces the Great Mosque built by 'Abd-ar-Rahman II as late as 825. This was related to La Mezquita in Córdoba but had only five aisles. The hump-backed churches on the sites of mosques as exemplified at Carmona occur here too. After the fall of the caliphate, the town was ruled by a governor and attained a degree of independence, only to fall to Ferdinand III of Castile in 1246. The town is situated in the midst of rich farmland and mulberry groves. It was known for its hot springs in Roman times and the Muslims built several *hammams*, of which the most magnificent was the Hammam ath-Thawr (Bath of the Bull).

Jaén: the old town has Islamic roots.

The monastery of San Domingo was once a Muslim palace, now gone without a trace. Very much alive is the **Palacio del Condestable** (Palace of the Constable), which was enriched by craftsmen from Granada. Of Jaén's churches, **La Magdalena** uses Roman tombstones, probably already part of the mosque which it replaced. **San Bartolomé**, also built on the site of a mosque, has fine wooden ceilings in the Granadine manner but is excelled by **Santa Clara**. **San Andrés** has some Mudéjar decoration. Among the eminent scholars born in Jaén was the poet al-Ghazal ('The Gazelle'), whom 'Abd ar-Rahman sent as ambassador to the Emperor Theophilus in Constantinople.

LAS NAVAS DE TOLOSA

Just south of the Desfiladero de Despeñaperros, a rugged mountain pass, notorious for bandits in times past, Las Navas de Tolosa, between Santa Elena and La Carolina, is

OTHER SITES NEAR JAÉN

The impressive castle of Baños de la Encina.

where the dying Muhammad ibn 'Abdullah ibn Nasir was defeated by Alfonso VIII in 1252. It was a moral victory for the Christians but the real defeat of the Almohads was by their own people at Marrakesh in 1269.

LINARES

From this junction of the railway a visit can be made to **Baños de la Encina**, the castle built by al-Hakam II between 967 and, possibly, as late as 986. It is an impressive mass, for the square-cut towers are double the height of the walls as if to let the sentries peer over the ridges of the hills. This castle was partly built to control an unruly province full of rough mountain fastnesses where any vagabond could gather a clan. The main gate is clamped between two towers as wide as itself and had doors, portcullis and machicoulis. It is heavily restored. This gate was the last of an old order which was to be superseded by the bent entry. The stonework is of royal quality.

MARTOS

The ruined castle of **La Peña** moulders on a precipitous height.

ÚBEDA

Here the mystic Juan de la Cruz died in 1591. Alfonso VIII took the town but could not hold it and it was taken again by Fernando III in 1234. The town walls have square towers and a 14th-century Mudéjar gate. The 13th-century **Puerta de Losal** has a double horseshoe arch. Note the toothed arch of the doorway of the church of **Santa Clara**.

MÁLAGA, ANDALUCÍA AND MURCIA

The old city of Málaga (*Malaka*) was set in the arc of the Bay of the Gibralfaro and the *rambla* (stream) running through it used to flood in the rainy season. The Phoenicians who founded the city were followed by the Romans, and the Byzantines came briefly. The quarry supplied marble for the greatest church in the world at that time, Sancta Sophia in Constantinople. The Visigoth Leowigild took the city in 571 and it was captured without difficulty by Tariq in 711. Here adherents welcomed 'Abd ar-Rahman I, the last of the Umayyads, who after landing at Almuñécar was on his way to Elvira. Finally, Ferdinand the Catholic took it in 1487 after a merciless siege which culminated in an *auto-da-fé* of the starved defenders.

In 1586, the remaining Muslims were expelled with renewed ruthlessness. The port for Granada, Málaga was known as an Earthly Paradise, a name given frequently by the poets to all Andalucía. Sweet waters refreshed it and the quarry was seemingly inexhaustible. Nonetheless, it suffered from several riots and uprisings. Málaga has never known a frost and its orchards have always been renowned, along with vineyards praised by Arab poets for the fine wines which they yielded. In the 19th century Málagan raisins were regarded as the finest, to the chagrin of Smyrna merchants. Sugar-cane was introduced along with apricots, once small and bursting with juice and aroma but now, like the town, swollen into something quite other.

The restored **Alcazaba** has an Islamic core. The monument had indeed been brought down onto its haunches, along with the footings of the stone houses which were within the walls. In essence, it was a true palace shaped like a parallelogram in the midst of a kite of protecting walls and towers. The entrance, protected by a monumental *albarrani* tower, admits to a small ante-hall, the beginning of one of the most elaborate of bent entrances. Turning the corner by all of 180 degrees the attacker was faced with two long and wide passages which narrow at their ends to turn again to confront yet another narrow door. This opens onto a large yard dominated by towers, including the noble **Torre de la Vela**. At the south end is yet another gate, La Puerta de las Columnas, opening into a second yard. Here a later gate was cut but the old route narrows into yet another corridor leading at last to the Arco del Cristo, which admits to the terrain round about the walls of the palace. Passing through the Puerta de Granada, the visitor reaches the miniature residence, which is a mixture of 11th- and 14th-century workmanship. The courts and their basins are more modest than the Alhambra and the horseshoe colonnades less elaborate. Some vaulting is pleasantly repainted but the walls are happily kept white for the imagination to decorate. An evocative serpentine stone channel transports one in the imagination down the Mediterranean to Middle Eastern lands faster than any magic carpet. It is now high and dry but shows how Islamic rulers liked to toy with water. Beyond a great cistern fed by a Cyclopean well are the *hammams* and beyond them is the **Puerta de la Torre del Homenaje** (Keep). Behind this is the entrance to the **Castillo del Gibralfaro** (Beacon on the Height), now made pretty with plants and trees, which is not what the builders had envisaged. The palace comprises an archaeological museum with Visigothic work and fine Islamic faience. The castle at the summit was remodelled in the Nasrid period with a walk along the double walls approached by a staircase which gives a depressing view of the ruthlessly redeveloped city. The walk ascends gradually to the Castillo itself where the light once flared, giving the castle its name. The **mosque** in the castle has been greatly altered but outside the precincts the **Puerta de los Atarazanas** (Gate of the Shipyard), built partly of marble by Yusuf I, still has its horseshoe arch. Once it admitted merchants to the wharf near the Puerta de Tetuán, for it was a defence against pirates of all nationalities. An inscription announces that God alone wins, which was the motto of the Nasrids, devout but defeatist. The Great Mosque has given way to the cathedral. It had five naves with five doors onto a courtyard.

MURCIA

The town was said to have been founded by the Muslims at the beginning of the eighth century, but it is clear that the Visigoths had a centre in the immediate locality and the re-use of Roman masonry implies that it existed even earlier. Murcia broke free of the Almohads, for it had always had a degree of independence under the Umayyads. In 1241 it was taken by Jaime I. The pre-eminent mystic Ibn 'Arabi was born in this town in 1165. The **cathedral** was built on the site of the Great Mosque and has obliterated all traces of it except that the windows at middle level are divided by colonnettes in the Muslim manner. The **Convento de Santa Clara** has Mozarabic grilles, but outside the town at the monastery of **La Noria**, whose name refers to the great irrigation wheels of the Arabs, one scents the great Islamic contribution to agriculture. The **Museo Arqueológico Provincial** holds a few Muslim relics but more Visigoth material. The 12th- to 14th-century walls were once remarkable and the **Puerta Santa Eulalia**, of Almohad construction, is unique in that its bent entrance branches both left and right.

ANTEQUERA (Nr Mocha)

This town was as large as Ronda in Islamic times and is likely to have been the first fortress in Spain to have withstood the use of gunpowder. The **Torre Mocha** is 13th-century and an Islamic fortification, although Washington Irving hedged his bets, wise man, and said that the castle was either Roman or Moorish. He would have been wiser to have said that it was both, with much else added later. It is strikingly different from other castles built by the Muslims because it is set on a low hill in the valley and because its long dumpy inner walls, together with the rectangular towers of the outer defences, appear more modest than they really are. The western **Puerta de Málaga** has Islamic horseshoe arches. The town was not taken by the Christians until 1410.

ARCHIDONA

The ruins of this fortress and the town walls do not compare with those of Antequera 14 km (9 miles) away. The **Santuario de la Virgen de la Gracia** was originally a mosque.

FUENGIROLA

This village's appearance of being untouched since Muslim times is deceptive. The 10th-century ruined castle is the hub of a string of towers along this coast, built to defend it against pirates.

MARBELLA
Some of the walls and the rebuilt 10th-century and later **Alcazaba** have more or less survived. There is a new mosque, the gift of King Faisal of Saudi Arabia.

MIJAS
This village was recently debauched by urbanization but the remains of an Arab castle are still there.

VELEZ MÁLAGA
There are substantial remains of an Arab castle and some of the original mosque in the church of **Santa María**, which has a good Mudéjar ceiling.

OTHER SITES
NEAR MURCIA

CARTAGENA *(Karta' janna)*
This ancient city known for its esparto grass was permitted to keep its bishop after the Muslim conquest. The town has the melancholy distinction of being the port from which the last of the Moriscoes were expelled from Christian Spain in the 17th century.

JUMILLA
The uncompromisingly plain Islamic castle is like a ship aground on the reef of crags above the town.

MONTEAGUDO
The outer suburb of Murcia was once Roman, and Roman stone was incorporated by the Arabs into the castle on its crag. It was in fact more of a fortified palace, as was discovered when it was partly excavated in 1924. It is now as ruined as a sandcastle washed over by the first wave, but it is possible to recognize the two inner concentric walks where once were rooms round the patio. Fragments of the rich decoration also remain but the patio was destroyed by a farmer who needed a cistern.

RONDA, ANDALUCÍA

From the eighth century onwards the emirate retained a degree of independence and a miniature but lively court flourished in Ronda. But finally in 1485 the last Islamic ruler was defeated by the new-fangled artillery, using cannon-balls for the first time, of Ferdinand of Aragón and Isabella of Castile (who gave birth to a daughter in a scraggy castle nearby during the siege). Until gunpowder was developed, Ronda had been impossible to capture, for the **Ciudad**, or township, is split from the suburbs by a ravine cleft by the

Ronda: the often rebuilt Puente Nuevo above the gorge.

River Guadalevín. The gorge winds but never narrows, so that the gap was always too great to span once the bridge was down. The inner town was further protected by taking refuge on the top of cliffs although nowhere was left simply defended by naked nature. The ramparts and towers include the advanced *albarrani* type. Below the **Alcazaba** is the massive **Puerta Almocábar,** with its horseshoe arch protected by huge salient towers. A curiosity is that the inner gate is not aligned with the outer although it does not form a bent entrance. To the west the horseshoe **Arco de Cristo** also survives. Once the main gate was forced an invader was faced by the *Alcazaba* on its peak.

At the opposite end of the Ciudad is the **Puente Nuevo** (New Bridge) which dates from the 18th century, whereas in the valley the **Puente Viejo** (Old Bridge), often repaired, still rides on horseshoe arches. This bridge leads along the track below the wall to the *hammam* which is one of the finest Muslim baths in Spain and also a beautiful interior space in its own right. It is situated in a walled garden by the river from which it drew its water and, although the site is unkempt, the atmosphere is agreeably rural. The barrel vaults are pierced with stars through which beams of light once trickled to irradiate the steam. All is brick and mortar within, including the bases and capitals of the octagonal piers which carry the horseshoe arches. The columns at each end of the three aisles are marble.

In the *Ciudad* is the **Casa del Rey Moro** (House of the Moorish King) — though probably in fact, the house of a less

Ronda: the *hammam* – the lights in its vaults are rather like portholes.

Ronda: Santa María la Mayor with the former minaret converted into a belfry.

august subject — which was restored over several centuries and finally rebuilt in the late 18th. It can be reached from the valley by a stairway which is said to have 365 treads — doubtless another is inserted in leap years. The **Casa de Mondragón** has two handsome patios and may replace an Islamic palace (where Ferdinand and Isabella stayed with their swaddled infant), but was rebuilt during the Renaissance and then cheerfully tiled. The third house which claims Islamic antecedents is the **Casa del Gigante**, built in the Mudéjar style. The courtyard retains the attributes of a modest Islamic palace. The **Colegiata de Santa María**

Ronda: the former minaret was the belfry of the vanished church of San Sebastián.

replaced the mosque and its mass dominates the *Ciudad* just as its predecessor did, like a liner among bumboats. The independent minaret has been much altered from two-thirds of the way up and now has a clock even more incongruous than the superstructure needed for the hanging of the bells. The tower stands handsomely four-square over the arched entry to the present church. In the vestibule fragments of the mosque decoration have been uncovered, including the *mihrab* itself. This simple niche now harbours an icon of the Virgin. There is also an inscription and one Islamic capital. In a square of its own is the **minaret** of another mosque, which was replaced by the lost church of San Sebastián. It is small but graceful, with a horseshoe arch over its door and two small twin windows over its midriff. These windows are not united by a lean column, as so often, but spaced apart within an inset panel. This attractive minor monument is in key with the winding alleys which open onto tiny plazas and sudden views across the immensity of plain and mountain.

OTHER SITES NEAR RONDA

ARDALES
The church of **Bobastro** is sign-posted by the reservoir. The fragmentary remains of the castle of Umar ibn Hafsun, built in 884, can be reached on its height above, while around it are the remains of a Muslim town which awaits excavation. The area is wild but the Encantada hills are singularly beautiful.

GAUCÍN
The ridge is split into two and on the loftier, romantic enough to captivate a Ludwig of Bavaria, is the castle of castles, which appears to date from the ninth century. Spurs of rock sustain this fortress from which the coast could be watched.

SETENIL
The remains of a castle and some walls suggest that this was a fortress and also a police outpost in the midst of a wild region. In the old *Ayuntamiento* is a fine wooden ceiling.

VALENCIA

The cathedral stands in place of the Friday Mosque. The **Torres de Serranos** dates from the end of the 14th century but the V-shaped formation of the stairs to the upper battlements is the descendant of those restored at the Aljafería in Zaragoza. There is little Mudéjar architecture but lavish plasterwork can be seen inside the **Palacio de Curiel de los Ajos**. At Valencia (*Balnasiyya*) the open-air court met to control the flow of the irrigation system fairly. The *Tribunal de las Aguas* (Water Court) still meets on Thursdays in front of the cathedral. In Muslim times it was one of several such visible courts of local government, among them the *Mesta* which regulated the migration and grazing rights of flocks and herds and which played a vital role after the reconquest in Andalucía, as in Castile and Extremadura, either preventing the enclosure of free pastures or abetting it, according to the degree of power the Crown could exert over the grandees.

ALCALÁ DE CHISVERT
Known also as **Castellón de la Plana**, the monumental Islamic castle retains its character even after the alterations which followed on the reconquest. The usual cubic plan is varied by extensive flanking walls which reflect the rocky terrain on which they ride.

BENASAL
The walled village dates from Muslim times. Either the inhabitants evaded expulsions or it was easy to repopulate in spite of its loneliness.

BUÑOL
The ruined Arab fortress once had François I for a prisoner.

CULLERA
There is a splendid eighth-century Muslim castle here and the **Torre de la Reina Mora** (Tower of the Moorish Queen) rises

OTHER SITES
NEAR VALENCIA

above the valley where once was the Muslim quarter.

JÁTIVA (*Shatiba*)

The town has few remains of its Islamic history except for the castle which commands the strategic road. It was founded before the coming of the Romans and the Arabs restored it extensively. It is built in and out of the rock as if playing hide-and-seek. Heavy restoration has now obliterated its sober forms of squat keep and towers and curtain walls and it wears the Gothic additions like fancy dress. Its strength is almost redundant, since the hardiest rock climber would have had difficulty in fighting after making the ascent; but fortifications are only valuable if they deter. The town was one of the first to be taken by the Arabs, in 714, and it prospered from the late ninth century, when it was far larger and more important than it is today. Jaime I of Aragón conquered it in 1240: all Muslims were rooted out in 1247. It was famous for its copious production of coarse paper, for which the Islamic cities had an insatiable appetite, and was probably the first centre of production in Europe. Water-marks have identified its export to all North Africa, from Morocco to Cairo. **San Bartolomé** replaced a mosque

Sagunto: the castle, which extends for a kilometre, stands above a Roman theatre.

which was an abutment to the defences of the city. The church has a notable wooden ceiling.

SAGUNTO

The castle is one of the largest in Europe and stands astride an inspiring height. The ashlar from the decayed Roman town was re-used by the Muslims and again later by the Christians. The castle was extensively altered over the years and machine-gun emplacements, turned turtle under shell-fire during the Civil War, are part of its tragic history. It fell apart and became distinct sections because of the need to straddle crags, making it difficult to maintain. Below it, the Roman amphitheatre was a perfect depot for ashlar. A fine horseshoe arch forms the gate to the **Plaza de Armas** and the **Puerta Ferrisa** is also Islamic. **Santa María** replaced the mosque.

TOLEDO AND CASTILLA LA MANCHA (NEW CASTILE)

Before venturing into New Castile, one should be aware that this region was a sparsely populated frontier world. Other than Toledo, the only towns that sprang up were rural settlements rather than centres of learning and interest: its heroes were closer to Billy the Kid than to Juan de la Cruz or Alfonso the Wise. It was the military knights, in particular the order of Santiago of Calatrava (whose headquarters at Calatrava la Nueva, Calzada de Calatrava, were a magnificent fortification with a huge round window like the moon) who organized life and the vast flocks and herds of the ranchers while excluding monks from the province. The red clay of La Mancha had precluded the growth of forests and the regions were notorious for their lack of water, exemplified in Mérida, for example, by the mudbanks of its river. It was a world of grass and raiding parties and a good breeding ground for *conquistadores*. Before the final capture of Granada the Castilian herdsmen were marketing their cattle and sheep in the Islamic towns and villages of Andalucía and leasing grazing land from the Muslims. The virtue of these mutually protective unions of shepherds and cattlemen was a sense of individual worth among the survivors. The democracy of the *Mesta* (see Valencia, p. 101), which the Christians took over, allowed routes and grazing grounds to be settled peaceably twice a year in order to make the trek from winter to summer pastures possible. Villages banded together so that the posse that defended the trekkers could be paid for fairly by each farmer. The officers, or *Alcaldes*, were regularly required to be replaced in order to frustrate the over-powerful from gaining the ascendancy. This system altered after the reconquest, but it was the most important contribution made by Berber traditions of grazing rights, born in the Atlas Mountains, to Christian Spain. The system was to cross to the New World. To arrive in Toledo, however, is to arrive above the tide of flocks and herds ever in motion. It can claim to have been one of the most civilized of all medieval cities before the reconquest and for some years after.

(*Opposite*) Toledo: the 12th-century Mudéjar Puerta del Sol.

105

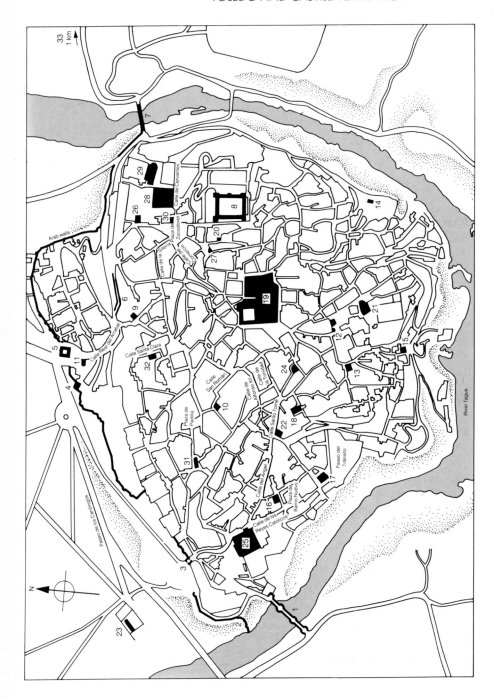

A car is of little use within the walls but is essential if this city is to be a centre, since public transport is limited. Once the Visigothic capital under the Muslims, Toledo (*Talaitula*) was sufficiently far from Córdoba to have a life of its own, and it achieved international eminence. The streets are narrow in the pursuit of the cool but the minds were neither. When it was reconquered in 1085 some Muslims and Jews remained and Raimondo, Archbishop from 1125 to 1151, also encouraged scholars from abroad to reside in the city. Translators worked on the Islamic texts, especially those concerned with the sciences. Robert Ketton translated the Qu'ran and several books on astronomy, to be rewarded with the Archdeaconship of Pamplona, and Gerard of Cremona resided there until he died in 1187. Toledo's civilizing influence spread as Jewish doctors left for the courts of Europe, among them Pedro Alfonso who served Henry I of England. Michael Scot deserted it for the pleasures of Sicily and to write books for the free-thinking Frederick II. Alfonso the Wise (1252–1284) sustained the scholarly tradition during his reign. The work on Arabic medicine, mathematics and metaphysics was to draw a ruffianly Europe out of the cesspool of the Middle Ages. There were also the refinements of Islamic cooking to digest. Toledo was famous for swords as well as scholarship and continues to make replicas as souvenirs for tourists.

(*Opposite*) Toledo
1. Puente de San Martín;
2. Baño de la Cava;
3. Puerta del Cambrón;
4. Puerta Alfonso VI;
5. New Bisagra Gate;
6. Puerta del Sol;
7. Puente de Alcántara; 8. Alcázar;
9. Cristo de la Luz; 10. San Román; 11. Santiago del Arrabal; 12. Santa Isabel de los Reyes; 13. San Bartolomé; 14. San Lucas;
15. San Sebastián;
16. Santa María la Blanca;
17. Sinagoga del Tránsito;
18. Taller del Moro;
19. Cathedral; 20. Torre de la Magdalena; 21. San Andrés; 22. Santo Tomé;
23. Cristo de la Vega;
24. Santa Ursula; 25. San Juan de los Reyes;
26. Convento de Santa Fé;
27. Corral de Don Diego;
28. Hospital de Santa Cruz;
29. Convento de la Concepción/San Jerónimo; 30. Arco de la Sangre del Cristo;
31. Santa Eulalia;
32. Santa Clara;
33. Casa de Galiana.

The Islamic frontier ran through Toledo from the Atlantic to Zaragoza. The sierra north-west of this line and north of the Ebro River formed a natural defence against the Christian states. Toledo was thus strategically situated as a border town, which is why watch-towers dot the line of hills to the north and the walls of the city were so fine.

On the western side of the city the walls descend the hill to meet the **Puente de San Martín**, dated 1203, so that, in one sense, it is a salient. Spanning the deep gorge of the Tagus, it was destroyed by a ferocious storm but was rebuilt in 1390 and repaired early in the 18th century. The two towered gates on each side were in the new-style Islamic manner. Just north of the bridge is the **Baño de la Cava**, a fortress tower to give even more protection, while the last tower of the walls paddles in the river. Northwards is the **Puerta del Cambrón** which was rebuilt, using the old *spoglia*, on the foundations

GATES AND WALLS

of the Arab Bab al-Maqabia, the original gate. Still built on rock, the walls lead eastwards, their stonework repaired in brick and the towers heavily rebuilt. Soon after the Puerta del Cambrón is a salient tower at the end of a mole which is equally high and with which it is totally integrated in the *albarrani* manner. A flourish of inappropriate flowers brings one to the noble **Puerta de Alfonso VI** or old Bisagra Gate through which the Christian monarch and the ambiguous hero, El Cid, entered the city in 1085. The flanking towers are little damaged by repair and floodlighting fixtures. Semi-circular, they thrust out beyond the gateway itself with its heavy stone voussoirs forming a horsehoe arch across which a prodigious monolith was laid to function, presumably, as a

The ninth-century Puerta de Alfonso VI or Old Bisagra Gate.

The Puente and
Puerta de Alcántara.

brace. There are imposts for a great door and grooves for a portcullis. Under the central vault are two bays; the one on the left hand may have been a secondary entrance to what is a miniature fortress. The sense of compactness is accentuated by the equal widths of each tower and the gate itself. Inside the walls the 12th-century Arab gatehouse was rebuilt in the 14th century as the Mudéjar **Puerta del Sol** (Sun Gate) with typical blind arcades and two contrasting horseshoe portals. The walls continue beyond the 16th-century New Bisagra Gate which is at once a simplified and amplified version of the old. Beyond it four towers in sequence serve as a lesson in degrees of repair or restoration. The first stands on its long rectangular blocks cut for the Romans with rough stonework rising to the battlements in coarse but orderly fashion, while the next tower has been botched together with cement. The walls now belly outwards to descend to the **Puente de Alcántara**, 866–871, with its two arches carrying it across the Tagus. Rebuilt in 1259 but on the original piers and restored twice again, it retains its dignity. The gate on the eastern shore is a baroque affair. The disparity between the span of the arches is in the Seljuq tradition of bridge building. They spring from rock to rock to avoid the expense of sinking piers into the river bed, while using as small a span as possible in order to conserve masonry. The gate on the city side is a cliff of stone towering over intruders while to the south there is a salient into the river. The inner gate is c.850 in date. Dr Juan Zazaya has argued that this, the **Bab al-Qantara** (Alcántara Gate) makes use of a bent entrance two centuries earlier than any other in Spain. The terrain is one reason: the traveller crossing the bridge passes through an arch 2 m (7 ft) wide into a vestibule which turns sharply to pass into a zigzag way leading up an uncompromising hillside into the city. Above is the **Alcázar**, the rebuilt fortress-palace of Toledo, which retains traces of its Islamic past.

CRISTO DE LA LUZ (The Mosque of Bab el-Mardum)

Dating from 999, the mosque was endowed by Musa ibn 'Ali. The interior is 6.5 m (21 ft) square and the central dome is 9.25 m (30 ft) high. The Visigothic church formerly on the site was demolished and materials from it, such as the capitals, still recognizable although their classical foliate decoration has been crushed by too firm a handshake, were re-used. The open hall was divided into nine compartments and the variations in the strapwork vaulting are Islamic in

The façade of Cristo de la Luz.

110

spirit. The delight in alternative vault construction is as if masons competed with each other to create ever more original and yet stable structures. The addition of the brick apse after 1085 has its own contrasting quality but the conversion obliterated the modest *mihrab* chamber which is now the south-east door, while the two original entrances are blocked out. When the little mosque stood alone like a

Cristo de la Luz: the interior open on three sides.

pavilion honouring death (since Islamic cemetery oratories often have open sides), nothing interfered with the light and shadows. Then, this metaphysical building must have had a quality that its loftiness and toughness can only partially convey today. Externally, the three horseshoe apertures on each side, their high encasing and rounded arches carrying a poetic arcade of three horsehoe arches with pink and white voussoirs after La Mezquita in Córdoba, are set with triple-lobed arches springing from slightly higher piers. The upper arches are of brick and the roof is carried on a double band of triangles under corbelled eaves in the Byzantine manner. The Mudéjar work round the apse is simpler but inoffensive.

SAN ROMÁN

The church of San Román survives its use as a museum of Visigothic Art. It was consecrated in 1221. Saints bowing under horseshoe arches are at once comic and touching. It is a nave-and-aisle church with alcoves and rooms which have lost their function along the south-east wall. Reredos apart, it is not like a Catholic basilica with the choir stranded amidships. The walls above the wide horseshoe arches are necessarily thin, else the broad arches could not have supported their weight, even though strengthened by piers. The capitals have strongly protruding curls of leaf as at Santa María la Blanca. The arcaded gallery has sets of triple arches. San Román is orientated north-east like so many of Toledo's churches. (San Pedro even points due north and San Salvador betrays a Muslim past by pointing south-east.) The south-east wall is a fine example of Mudéjar decoration, like a splendid carpet. The slim windows crowned by triple-lobed horseshoe arches have interlacing stars which might have come from Damascus. The timber ceiling is simple. There is one fine tower for a belfry.

SANTA MARÍA
LA BLANCA

The garden with its shade and subdued exterior precede the white vision inside this former synagogue. After the expulsion of the Jews it could have been given to no one else save the Virgin. Four rows of arches spring from octagonal piers with capitals like fishnets full of fir cones; they curve into each other, giving a swing to the rhythm of the arcade. Above are two patterns of interlace with intervals of white plaster

Santa María la Blanca: the piers temporarily stripped of plaster to reveal the brickwork.

between. The thin delineation is effeminate but not the big sun grilles. The gallery arcade recalls that of San Román and the dark timber ceiling emphasizes the lightness below. Curiously, one feels closer to a North African mosque here than in any other building in Toledo. The first synagogue on this site was rebuilt in 1250 on its 12th-century foundations and appropriated by the Christians in the 15th century. Misused by both time and its use as a carpenters' workshop, it is now well restored.

A Serpentine tree of life in the Mudéjar Sinagoga del Tránsito.

SINAGOGA DEL TRÁNSITO

The synagogue was built in 1357 by Mudéjar masons for the Treasurer of Castile, Simon Levi, who served Pedro the Cruel but was executed by him. The monumental empty prayer hall is 23 m (75 ft) long by 9.5m (31 ft) wide and 17 m (56 ft) high. Its pretty pavement is inset with tiles and its carved ceiling carries a fine Arabic inscription. An upper arcade of seven lobed arches runs before the plaster windows in the form of triple suns. It is bounded by a clear, rhythmic Hebraic inscription below which Islamic and Hebrew inscriptions and the coats-of-arms of Castile and León are intermixed among a frieze of branches of a tree of life. The once-coloured stucco interlace panels combine Christian and Islamic motifs that must have been taken from those of the brocaded silks for which Toledo was famous. The synagogue is an embryonic museum of Hebrew culture and includes archives and a library.

THE CATHEDRAL

Inside, the external wall of the Capilla Mayor has, among niches hidden in foliage, a Gothic carving of Abu Walid who, after the reconquest, prevented turmoil by assigning the Great Mosque to the visitors. The octagonal chapel of Ildefonso might almost be a vast *mihrab* while in the Chapter House is a Mudéjar coffered ceiling encumbered with gold.

The 14th-century church of **San Bartolomé** is one of a group with brick-tiered apses.

The Mozarabic church of **San Lucas** has a *plaza* all to itself with just enough room for three children to swing on old car tyres. Tower and garden charm. The plan was distorted to fit the site.

Although of seventh-century origin, the church of **San Sebastián** is 16th-century. In the quarter of the Mozarabs, it rides above the Tagus gorge and the weir. It has kept its Visigothic columns and handsome horseshoe arches.

The graceful tower of **Santa Isabel de los Reyes** contrasts with the Arab door which has a cross-beam on consoles under its gothic arch. Both tiers of apse arches are cusped and lively. Inside, there is late *azulejo* work on a north-west side altar, while the ceiling is inventive with the effect of woven cradles between cross-beams.

Santiago del Arrabal, *c*.1265, has Mudéjar triple apses with monumental tiers of arcades, the brickwork tempered by time. The rectilinear frieze of the lateral door is related to that of Cristo de la Luz, while the porch on the south side is sober. The late 12th-century tower beside it is equally severe. The interior is spacious under brick vaulting and holds a Gothicized Mauresque pulpit. Below the church is a group of wood and amber-painted plaster houses of some antiquity but no certain date.

No true workshop ever had the palatial rooms, horseshoe arches and extravagant height which mark this Mudéjar palace, or so one would think. Yet here indeed was the workshop where masons, many of them Muslim by birth, recut stone from the Friday Mosque for the cathedral which replaced it in the 13th century. Master masons also came from France to carve the splendid statuary of that holy house. The hall is 16.2 m (53 ft) long by 7.35 m (24 ft) wide and is attended by smaller rooms on either side; it is purely Arab in feeling. Lavish plasterwork frames the great doors, the archways and windows. Above elaborate friezes, wooden ceilings evolve into webs of stars and octagons. The museum holds tiles from many periods and a delectable box, a vine-clad font and two Ali Baba pots swathed in inscriptions and decorations.

TALLER DEL MORO (Workshop of the Moor)

MINOR MONUMENTS

San Andrés has a Mozarabic ceiling and **San Tomé** a Mudéjar tower as do **San Cipriano, San Miguel** and **San Pedro Martín**. La **Magdalena** has been rebuilt, however. The **Ermita del Cristo de la Vega** has a fine tiered apse but the Mudéjar **Santa Úrsula** was manhandled in the 16th century. The many styles of **San Juan de los Reyes** are hard to unravel. One exterior serves as a hatstand from which hang the chains worn by Christian prisoners. The cloisters have wooden vaults with small stars between grand planets. The **Convento de Santa Fé** has one octagonal room, showing that a Muslim mansion is buried here. One of its interlace arcades is related to that of Cristo de la Luz and another is transitional from horseshoe to Gothic. The apse is divided into panels by buttresses, a link with the Visigothic and Mozarabic past. The **Corral de Don Diego** also has one octagonal room. The **Hospital de Santa Cruz** has bits and pieces from the Islamic period in its museum while the courtyard has Visigothic columns and capitals and handsome ceilings. Below it, the **Convento de la Concepción Francisco** is a village of additions anchored by its tower. The dome of its Mudéjar **Capilla de San Jerónimo** has 15th-century tiles in the ribbed star of its dome which outside is hemispherical and unexpectedly covered in lead in the Ottoman manner.

The **Plaza de Zocodover**, shaped like the head of a halberd, was the centre of town. It began as the *Suq ad-Dawab* or horse market, which drew buyers from far and wide. In it is the **Arco de la Sangre del Cristo** (Arch of the Blood of Christ) which is a red brick rebuilding of a vast, appropriately horseshoe, arch. The **Capilla de San Lorenzo** has little waves of cusped arches within a powerful horseshoe. **Santa Eulalia** also has horseshoe arches both outside and in, and the tower displays many textures from the worn plush of the brick to the abrasiveness of hewn stone. The **Convento de Santa Clara la Real** contains the Patio de los Laureles with horseshoe arches confined to the ground level.

BEYOND THE WALLS

Excavations have revealed the **Casa de Galiana**, a 13th-century palace, now richly and scrupulously restored. The enclosure measures 23.75 m (78 ft) by 14.4 m (47 ft) and holds a patio with a nest of arcaded halls and a wide stairway to the former upper floor. There are three cusped horseshoe windows although the rest are semi-circular with brick voussoirs. Rough-hewn blocks of stone are set between belts of brick.

ALARCÓN
The Mudéjar tower of **San Pedro** is a fine octagonal example among a number of neglected churches.

ALARCOS
Nuestra Señora de Alarcos on the hill mourns the battlefield where the Muslims destroyed the forces of Alfonso VIII, the last major defeat for the Christian armies. The Almohad leader Yusuf crossed the Straits with a large army and razed the town to the ground. Only 300 cavalry escaped and the country was laid waste as far as Toledo. The hills still harbour wolves, boar and red deer and, allegedly, bandits. Here, ironically, Moorish units were sent to round up Republican partisans after the Civil War.

ALBACETE
The town was founded by Arabs and there are remnants of the walls. In 1145 and 1146 it was the scene of ferocious fighting against Christian invaders. The land around it was an estate of Boabdil (see pp. 62–3); after the fall of Granada he was allowed to settle with his hawks and greyhounds at Andarax, only to be uprooted after seven years when Don Juan of Austria quelled a local uprising and the last Muslims were expelled from Spain. By way of revenge, they are said to have helped Ottoman corsairs raid the coast, but Albacete, which is far from the sea, seems an unlikely cradle to produce navigators in any number.

ALCALÁ DE HENARES (*al-Qala' an-Nahr*)
The restorations after the disastrous fire of 1940 include the walls and the palace of the archbishop where the façades are in a medley of styles, one of which is Mudéjar-Gothic. The last trace of the Muslim-Christian conflict is the ruin of Alcalá la Vieja beyond the suburbs. The town is honoured as the birthplace of Cervantes in 1547 whose great Don Quixote laughed chivalric posturing off the stage of Spain.

OTHER SITES IN CASTILLA LA MANCHA (NEW CASTILE)

CALATRAVA LA VIEJA
The Muslim ruins here are the most important being researched now. The *albarrani* tower was projected to control and protect the water-wheel which is part of an elaborate moat and quarry for the inner town and palace. Pure water was drawn from the river above the moat while waste water was carried away by the lower stream. Excavations show that the town spread far beyond the walls.

CARDENETE
Possesses little except the 42 m (138 ft)-long ceiling of its church: it is enough.

CIUDAD REAL
The town has a fine Mudéjar gate with a horseshoe arch between two towers. The town was given to the knights of Santiago of Calatrava who were the defence against the Muslims. Later, their usefulness gone, the knights fell into disgrace and the domain was taken back by Alfonso the Wise.

MADRID (*Majrit*)
Madrid was one of the four fortresses which the Arabs established across the Iberian peninsula from Elvira in Portugal through Badajoz to Zaragoza. It was reconquered by Alfonso VI of León. Below the new cathedral, ever building, is all that remains of the Islamic fortifications, which are interesting for anyone studying masonry techniques. Madrid is a good centre but has few Islamic elements apart from its great museum collections (see page 146). **San Pedro** has a plain Mudéjar tower built of pink brick. The 'Moorish' quarter and the former *Judería* (Jewish quarter) have been ruthlessly developed. The *louche* atmosphere of the Plaza Mayor, with its musicians, beggars and strolling youth, has something of the atmosphere of an African *maidan* about it in spite of splendid Renaissance architecture.

MAQUEDA
The 15th-century castle has a Mudéjar gate and the church below an apse similar in style. **Santa María** is inextricably mixed up with the Islamic town walls. Its side entrance is approached by steps, once a slope, between two towers and was formerly the town gate. The blocked machicoulis is

still there, as are the grooves for the portcullis and the supports for the massive door.

MELQUE

The archaeological museum in Madrid has important material on, and a model of, this Mozarabic church. It is grand in its dimensions and in the size of its stones. Considerably restored after excavation, it remains a moving seventh-century monument. The central crossing has a squat tower with rooms each side of the sanctuary, additions which break the restrained simplicity of having one window to each stretch of wall. The central piers supporting the dome are coupled and rounded, as are the outside corners of the building. The sanctuary ends in a horseshoe-shaped room which could have been a forerunner of the *mihrab* of La Mezquita, Córdoba. The rhythm of the external stonework has been altered by restoration but where it is intact there is a pattern of groups of headers and stretchers which recalls Armenian masonry.

MOLINA DE ARAGÓN

This busy town possesses a wrecked Christian castle which appears to have been built, in part at least, by Muslim masons in the 12th to 13th centuries. The keep on the height with curtain walls is part of a grand scheme of fortifications on far-flung outcrops of rock. Three outstanding towers built in the Islamic tradition of ashlar cornerstones with rubble infill appear to stagger above the town, grey framed in red.

SIGUENZA

The rebuilt *Alcázar* (now a Parador) had been much altered when it became the palace of the bishops. It is matched by the grey towers of the cathedral, mid-12th-century, which reminds one that one is nearer to France than Andalucía. In it is a notable collection of fabrics.

TALAMANCA

The Islamic walls are mid-ninth-century and, with their use of mixed brick and stone, are related to those of Madrid.

TALAVERA DE LA REINA

There are four Mudéjar churches: **San Miguel** of the 12th century, much altered; **Santiago de los Caballeros**, 13th-

Talavera de la Reina: the projecting or *albarrani* tower.

century; 14th-century **San Pedro**, altered beyond recognition, and **Santiago**, Mudéjar-Gothic, with a highly decorated tower and the most interesting of the group. **San Francisco** also has a Mudéjar tower. Some walls and *albarrani* towers are noteworthy examples because lofty and complete with machicoulis in their arches. One stretch gives an impression of the defensive system with the first tower arch pointed and the other two horseshoe in form. There are vestiges of other square towers between them. One polygonal tower, topped by very late battlements, may originally have been round. The stone is Roman, especially the large ashlar blocks at ground level. Voussoirs of stone alternating with brick layers give the patterned effect common to Islamic work. The stone is carefully laid on the diagonal but, as with Visigothic masonry, headers are paired or grouped to punctuate the passage of the courses. There are stones cased in brick in the Byzantine manner and also brick repairs. Where brick is decorative, there Mudéjar begins. Across the town two more *albarrani* towers comingle with houses.

TORRIJOS
The mansion of the Duques de Altamira was built by Juan de Herrera in the Muslim style with interlacing, arabesque décor and fine ceilings.

CASTILLA Y LEÓN
(OLD CASTILE)

ÁGREDA
The castle of La Muela is as ruined as the town walls which were Roman but added to by the Arabs. The site is bounded by a precipice.

ARÉVALO
Castles can sometimes look like silos but the castle here was really used as such. The town is one of the birthplaces of the Mudéjar style. The 13th-century brick towers of **San Martín** are as grand as they are restrained. The 13th-century **Convento de Nuestra Señora de la Lugareja**, although never finished, shows the gamut of brick decoration evolving into a coherent composition. **San Miguel** was rebuilt in the 15th century but preserves some of its Mudéjar decoration inside, while a 16th-century revival of the style can be seen in **San Salvador**. There are two bridges in the Mudéjar style.

BERLANGA DE DUERO
Seven km (4 miles) outside the village is the 12th-century square Mozarabic church of **San Baudelio**, famous for its frescoes which were stolen in the 1920s but have now been returned from New York, faded but poignant. As if an Armenian or a Mughal architect had been employed, the roof supports radiate from a central column. Although the church measures but 8.5 × 7.5 m (28 × 25 ft) the gallery is supported on 16 piers bearing horseshoe arches. The effect is of some esoteric cult chamber. 15 km (9 miles) from Berlanga is **Gormaz**, among the greatest of Islamic fortresses, which dates from 960. It is related to the castles of Baños de la Cerrata, Guadix and Zorita de los Canes but the forebear of the gate is to be found at Tarifa. Shaped like a ploughshare to fit the razorback ridge, Gormaz has some 25 towers and an angled entrance.

BURGOS
The **Convento de Las Huelgas** was founded in 1187 by Alfonso VIII to please his wife Eleanor, daughter of Henry II

Burgos: the Arco de
San Martín built in the
10th century.

of England. The great cloister doors are Almohad workmanship. The Capilla de la Asunción is over-exotic. Prettier is the
Capilla de Santiago standing all alone in the garden and
entered through a brick horseshoe arch. The museum has a
collection of fabrics mainly from the 13th and 14th centuries.
Note the city gateway, known as the Arco de San Esteban.

CUELLAR
San Esteban has an elaborately decorated brick apse and
fine Mudéjar plaster tombs. **San Salvador** is another early
Mudéjar church. They exemplify the Romanesque and
Mudéjar styles in Old Castile. The 13th-century **San Nicolás
de Bari** is a formative Mudéjar building with a handsome
tower. **Santa María del Castillo** has a Mudéjar apse.

GORMAZ (*see* BERLANGA DE DUERO)

MADRIGAL DE LAS ALTAS TORRES
The town is famous for its walls and lofty towers. **San Nicolás
de Bari** is a formative Mudéjar building and **Santa María
del Castillo** has a Mudéjar apse.

MAYORGA DE CAMPOS
A cradle of the Mudéjar style, to be seen in churches such as
Santa María de Arbas and **Santa Marina**.

MEDINACELI (*Madinat Salim* — Salim's Town)

Al-Mansur died in the *Alcazaba* which was then transformed into the palace of the dukes who, in the curious manner of Spanish grandees, took their titles from Muslim strongholds, just as British generals also liked to do. **San Román** was a synagogue.

OLMEDO

The 12th-century walls and gates still stand but the town is remarkable for the Mudéjar churches of **San Miguel, San Andrés** and the decayed chapel of the **Convento de la Mejorada.**

QUINTANILLA DE LAS VIÑAS

Outside the village, the Visigothic church of **Nuestra Señora de las Viñas** dates from the seventh century but with later additions. A magnificent horseshoe arch dominates the sanctuary of this once three-aisled church and the reliefs are vivid. The masonry is Roman *spoglia* and the Visigoths chose the largest, as if breaking backs saved time.

SAN CEBRIÁN DE MAZOTE

The triple-aisled Mozarabic church is restored. Dating from the beginning of the tenth century, it has a horseshoe-plan sanctuary facing an even larger horseshoe chapel at the far end of a nave five arches long. The transepts end with curved walls. The crossing is a dramatic encounter between longitudinal and transversal horseshoe arches. The church feels larger than it is and the interior is unexpectedly light.

SEGOVIA

The town, which was in the hands of the Muslims until 1085, was the prosperous centre of the weaving industry. The **Alcázar** rides on an outcrop above the muddled streets of the former Islamic quarter; its foundations can be traced along the surface of the rock but the jolly turrets and grand-opera massing of the masonry date from after the reconquest. **San Lorenzo** has a Mudéjar tower and **San Millán** a triple apse and a Mudéjar ceiling. Tenth-century **San Martín** was rebuilt in the 12th, leaving Mozarabic traces.

SORIA

San Juan de Rabanera has a Byzantine dome structure,

while the interlace patterns in **San Juan de Duero** are Islamic. Both churches date from *c.*1200. The latter has a curious courtyard which gives the impression that it is 90 degrees out of true. The arcades are half rounded Romanesque and half crossed and looped horseshoe Mudéjar arches.

TORDESILLAS
The former palace of Pedro the Cruel, now the **Convento de Santa Clara**, displays the full magnificence of the Mudéjar style which he liked so much. Horseshoe arches, freestanding or forming blind arcades, predominate, while the patio and the great rooms with patterned moulded plaster have all the Mudéjar plastic attributes. A fine example of a *hammam* was built here.

VALLADOLID
The **Colegio de San Gregorio** has a Mudéjar window in its courtyard and the **Hospital de Esquera** a Mudéjar ceiling. The **Palacio de María de Molina** boasts a huge horseshoe archway and the **Palacio de Tordesillas** has a patio which is exotically Islamic in atmosphere. The buildings of the **Capilla Dorada**, however, ended up entangled in their own coarse interlace.

OTHER SITES IN CASTILLA Y LEÓN WITH VISIGOTHIC AND MOZARABIC MONUMENTS

Alba de Tormes: some Mudéjar work.
El Campillo (near Zamora): the fine Visigothic San Pedro de la Nave.
Peñalba de Santiago: Mozarabic church.
Ponferrada: 10th-century Mozarabic San Tomas de las Ollas.
Sahagún: Mudéjar San Tirso.
Toro: 13th-century Mudéjar San Salvador, San Pedro and others.

MÉRIDA AND EXTREMADURA

Mérida was a town of sheep breeders whose fame rests on the supposition that they bred the Merino strain which was to spread across all Europe. Now it is mildly prosperous and has a monumental new Roman Museum. The town is a good centre and is the tourist capital of this province, discussed briefly in relation to New Castile.

The extensive Roman remains which survived quarrying include the magnificent **bridge** and the aqueduct which may possibly have influenced the structure of La Mezquita, Córdoba. The 130 m (425 ft)-square **Alcazaba**, with elements from many periods since the Roman, was greatly altered by 'Abd ar-Rahman II in 835, using Syrian building techniques and much Roman masonry. The gatehouse under restoration was added to control the bridge across the mudbanks of the Guadiana. Recent work has exposed a plethora of walls and foundations. Modern work includes concrete underpinning of the riverside walls. Square corner bastions and square towers between them show some Byzantine influence. Massive towers flank the gate and, as so often with Arab defences, each is the same width as the entry. They rise level with the castellated walls which are 2.7 m (9 ft) thick. They may have been the first site where the

Mérida: Puente Romano from the Alcazaba walk.

125

(*Left*) Mérida: the stairway leading to the well.

(*Right*) Mérida, Alcazaba: re-used Visigoth materials in the entrance to the well.

concept of the outflung tower was realized, but the controversy over the origins of the *albarrani* defence system cannot be resolved here. Nonetheless, these extended towers joined by an arch reaching the same level represented an important advance in military engineering. In the enclosure is the most famous cistern in Spain. The water flows in directly from the river down a vaulted tunnel carried on Visigothic pilasters and over a bed of ashlar. A double staircase leads to the water's edge, one for ascent and one for returning with the emptied buckets. There is some foliate decorative spoglia and an inscription to Ja'far whose father was a slave freed by 'Abd ar-Rahman II.

The church of **Santa Eulalia** is a noble building and retains Visigothic elements which include part of the southeast porch and twin windows above the sanctuary.

The **Visigoth Museum** has two fascinating examples of architectural perspective, achieved by means of columns, and in another alcove are a pair of 'Wild Men' from a former palace.

OTHER SITES IN EXTREMADURA

ABADÍA

Near the attractive village of Hervás, this hamlet grew round the abbey, later a palace. It has a Mudéjar cloister, including a composite of octagonal piers and broad capitals embossed with leaf forms. These carry uniquely elongated horseshoe arches with voussoirs picked out in brick. Each arch is also framed in brick.

AZUAGA

The Islamic castle was enlarged after the reconquest but is now in ruins. A horseshoe gate between round towers survives.

BADAJOZ

This is the tragic capital of Extremadura and not a centre for tourists. It is set in the middle of a marshy plain and narrow streets rise sharply above the broad Guadiana River which loafs its course along. The **Plaza Alta** has been cleared of squatters; the fine whitewashed square with its arcades has but the shells of houses which await their fate. The castle was a key fortification in the border defence system. Its bent entrance was an important 12th-century innovation and the horseshoe arch is very grand indeed. At a whim, the builder inserted an acanthus capital as a decoration above the gate. The castle, with its rambling walls, has been so smartened up as to be dateless, while the old museum is abandoned. The castle was taken by the Almoravids in 1094 and by Alfonso IX in 1229. Originally the palace of a Visigoth bishop, it was partly rebuilt in the Mudéjar style. The towers include some which appear to be early examples of the *albarrani* type. In the midst of decay, the **Torre Espantaperros** built by the Almohads *c.*1150 stands as a humbler kinsman of the Torre del Oro of Sevilla. In the **Plaza de la Soledad** down the hill is a pretty example of Mudéjar revival architecture with a miniature Giralda tower: a department store, it is closed and its fate is in the balance, as is that of one or two modest Art Nouveau buildings. The massive cloister of the **cathedral** must possess more 16th-century *azulejos* than anywhere else in Spain.

Near the city is the battlefield where in 1086 Alfonso encountered Yusuf, the emir of the Almohads, once a Christian slave who, even in old age, toothless and with a quavering voice, inspired his followers with his zest and unwavering devotion to his austere beliefs. But there were other aspects of his character. Before the battle he had left his youngest son sick in Sevilla and when at noon there was a lull in the fighting he wrote a poem assuring the boy that even in the midst of the fray his heart remembered him. When night fell, his victory was complete. Such a man could hardly lose.

CÁCERES

The walled inner town is spectacular with palaces and the streets and shapeless plazas follow the rugged contours of rocks that are exposed in places. Above the Arco del Cristo is a heavily restored Arab house. Mudéjar elements abound — in particular in the **Calle Aldano** where one twin window is a ghost in the wall but where there are several extant examples. No. 14 has a striking brick façade. The lane extends into the **Calle del Olmos** where there are handsome stone versions. The Arab fortifications have been altered continually and the **Alcázar** rebuilt as a Renaissance palace, the **Casa de las Veletas**, now the excellent museum. It retains a cistern which is 13.4 m (44 ft) by 9.9 m (32 ft). Its 16 columns are less than two metres high but the horseshoe arches reach a height of 3.35 m (11 ft) and are strikingly large, while the barrel vaulted ceilings are lofty, especially when seen from the peephole window in the gallery above the cistern. The ginger-tinted walls were Roman but altered by the Muslims who extended several *albarrani* towers, two at least having been repeatedly altered. The Torre Rodonda is elegantly octagonal with two piers supporting a stair. The walls are of *tapia*, a concrete of mortar and small stones. Restoration here is severe, so that

Cáceres: a typical pair of Islamic windows.

(*Above*) Cáceres: the cistern in the basement of the Casa de las Veletas (now the museum).

(*Right*) Garrovillas: the lurching arcades of the village centre.

the Espadro tower stands exposed opposite the rebuilt Toledo-Moctezuma palace.

GARROVILLAS
The lurching arcades of the plaza suggest a Muslim past. It is one of the more picturesque of the weaving villages of this region.

GRANADILLA
The village was deserted and although walled has no towers. A remarkable keep was added after the reconquest.

GUADALUPE
The renowned monastery was a stronghold but is without trace of the Arab occupation, which began as early as 712. The Templete (or Chapel) in the midst of a cloister is a masterpiece of Mudéjar architecture. This square sanctuary is Gothic and develops in three stages, two octagonal and one hexagonal, as if tiered ruffs round the spire which finally peaks above them. Its brickwork is lacelike under the firm waves of the eaves; tiles add colour. The cloister has two tiers of horseshoe arches. The upper ranks carry the eaves, above which are paired windows. The corners of the parapets gallery are cut away to hold octagonal cisterns.

HORNACHOS
The castle has a polygonal tower and extensive ruins of widespread curtain walls which suggest that they contained the nucleus of the Islamic town.

JEREZ DE LOS CABALLEROS
The walls are mostly Islamic but the castle was built by the Templars. The town stands on two hills with the church of **San Miguel** on the ridge between. Its massive brick tower combines as many styles as ingredients in a Christmas cake. The tower of **San Bartolomé** is the baroque answer to La Giralda but has horseshoe elements; big glazed roundels and rectangles appear to button it together. The white town, turned in on itself with its narrow alleys, seems detached from the world. It was here that the Templars were disbanded because of their misdeeds. Attacked by their own monarch in 1311, the last defenders came to grief in the Torre Sangrienta. The blood was their own.

LLERENA
Part of the Arab walls still cuddle this small town which is dominated by the tower of **Nuestra Señora de la Granada**, with its double-tiered arcades.

MONTÁNCHEZ
A handsome small town dominated by the large ruined **Alcázar**, of which some towers are still standing. It was largely built with Roman materials but it is not clear where earlier fortifications stood. The *Alcázar* is little altered, except for the addition of a shrine with *azulejo* work which could have pagan antecedents. The considerable cisterns suggest that it was a refuge for the townsfolk.

PORTEZUELO
This large Muslim castle was extended after the reconquest.

TRUJILLO
The town lies beneath a fine Islamic castle, possibly ninth-century in date, but extended by the Almohads. It always had a series of towers but the Almohads may have added the *albarrani* towers, one of which extends 9m (30 ft) from a curved wall tower but is only 2.6 m (7 ft) wide and reaches a forward tower 5m (16 ft) square. Trujillo fell to Ferdinand III of Castile in 1232 and it was then that the statue of the Virgen de la Victoria was set up and the castle altered. The town was given to the Knights of Trujillo to defend since the reconquest was not secure. The large plaza recalls those of North Africa because it was originally free in form. In a corner is **San Martín** with a square tower, likely to have been a minaret, and a slender clock tower. **Santa María la Mayor** replaces the Great Mosque. Bits of the old walls can be found including the **Arco de San Andrea**. Lanes meander as they did in Muslim times.

ZAFRA
The **Alcázar** was remarkable for its lofty walls incorporated in the palace of the Duque de Feria, ambassador to London. It is now a Parador but retains an amazing octagonal ceiling in fretwork.

ZARAGOZA AND ARAGÓN

Zaragoza is famous for its nuts; here a memorable dish of walnuts and cream with the tang of honey, invented by Ziryab (see p. 43) is still served. Sadly, there is the tang of demolitions in the old town within the broad roads that have replaced its walls. New apartments have blocked the skyline and they hem in even the Aljafería, once the suburban estate of the Berber emir. Berbers ruled a population of some 17,000 from the eighth century but they were clans from the hills and not city dwellers. If they were puritanical, they do not appear to have stopped dancing, for if you see the *Jota* you are close to Muslim Spain. Urban life triumphs over the pastoral in the end, however; the Banu-Hud emirs were poets who mixed Arab and Berber romance into something other than the songs of Andalucía.

In the eighth century, egged on by the Abbasid caliph in Baghdad, the emir broke his bond with Andalucía but lost his nerve and asked Charlemagne for help. When it came in 777, he immediately repented and shut the gates of the city in the face of the emperor, who was then recalled to Germany. Legend tells how his retreating army was massacred by the Basques at Roncevalles, where Roland sounded his horn for the last time. After years of intermittent siege the city finally fell to the Christian armies in the early 12th century, but evidence of Mudéjar culture all over Aragón shows how the Berbers and their unveiled women adapted and prospered under their new rulers.

THE ALJAFERÍA

Philip II encircled the palace with Renaissance defences which foreshadowed the redoubts of Vauban. The front part of these was pulled down in the 19th century, leaving an imprint on the ground; hydrants and hoses took the place of guns. Approached from the front the extensively rebuilt pink façade is impressive and the restored brick castellations are in keeping with it. Casts were taken from material kept at the Archaeological Museum in Madrid in order to restore the decoration in plaster, and the results are satisfactory. The

Zaragoza, the
Aljafería: an exercise
in geometry – the
gate, towers and
keep of the palace.

gateway between two close-set towers is bound by a
horseshoe arch which is set within one still grander. There is
a parade of Gothic arches formed by crossed semi-circular
blind arches above the door. Higher still is the open arcade
of a walk or belvedere and over all looms the formidable
keep with five arrow slits in each flank. The composition is not
dully symmetrical: the two corner towers are shorter than the
others and the arrow slits vary in number. There is modern as
well as Renaissance work in the entry court and a church
occupies the possible site of the garrison mosque. The
galleries for defence include a double stairway which was to
be copied in Valencia. An arcade presents a glimpse of
patios but the entry is oblique and through a forehall.
Immediately upon entering the precinct of the sovereign his
exquisite oratory welcomes strangers. The leaping arches
under the dome derive from Córdoba, while two more on
each side at gallery level have five-lobed arches, forerunners of the later mosque of Tinmal in Morocco. The
arcade at floor level has interlace scrolling and leaves in
deep relief over the rest of the wall. Short columns support
consoles knotted by floral bands. These cross the corners of
a square room to make it seem octagonal. One deeper
alcove inset beyond a horseshoe arch is the *mihrab*. There
are alternating voussoirs of marble and carved stone
supported on twin free-standing columns. All the capitals are
vegetal. The half-dome within the *mihrab* is ribbed and on its
way to becoming a scallop shell, with all its traditional

Zaragoza, the Aljafería: the mystical calm of the hall with the pool.

symbolism of security.

Between the oratory and the second court a mystical pool lies in the shadows. Some of the arches of the second court have 11 lobes and 10 sharp teeth while two manage 17 lobes. Other arcades have arches with elaborate interlacings which flow over a band of upper arches in defiance of structural rules; all weigh down on free-standing coupled columns at ground level. As at Córdoba, the problem was one of re-using existing columns which were too short and the multitude of decorative elements above compensates for this, as it dances before your eyes. In the far arcade three pairs of columns are planted amid the market garden of the strapwork. The capitals are vegetal or plain but have no colour. The end hall is now bare behind two magnificent doorways. That on the right leads to the keep and battlements. In front of this royal hall is the marble pavement of the **Hall of the Orator**. Beyond this is yet another chamber with a long pool under a plain ceiling, all the original ones having been lost. To step out from this cool retreat is to reach the court and its sunken garden. Its flanks are arcaded; one with plain but the other with lobed arches. On the right is a Renaissance stair built for Ferdinand and Isabella. At the far end with a flourish of interlacing are leap-frogging arches on columns and piers. A marble ramp with tiny fountains leads to a second rectangular pool and to where were once the vanished apartments added in the 11th century under Abu Ja'far Ahmad. The gallery looking onto this court has barley-

Zaragoza, the Aljafería: elaborate arcading which has been carefully restored.

twist columns by Renaissance confectioners. The broad staircase was grand enough for the Emperor Charles V to walk up and has a vast wooden ceiling. A richer example covers the throne-room on the upper floor where there is a curiously high gallery. It was a palace with as many details as there are leaves in a forest: every voussoir is carved and every brick plastered.

THE CHURCHES

La Seo, the old cathedral, is in disarray. The apse preserves its Mudéjar framework into which Gothic windows fit less happily than those from the Romanesque period beneath them. Under the eaves are townscapes of little villas masquerading as castellations. The interweaves descend from Roman mosaic work and hang like rugs. This filigree work in brick covers the walls of the Barroquieta Chapel. How remarkable the cathedral must have been before Gothic mutilated the Romanesque period. Islamic capitals have been found in the building and the carved door of the sacristy is outstanding Mudéjar work. The ruins exposed in the dishevelled plaza in front of La Seo are Roman.

The rival baroque cathedral of **Nuestra Señora del Pilar** is Andalucían Mudéjar but is the precursor of too many *hôtels de ville*. Externally it might remind an alcoholic of the Kremlin.

San Gil has very delicate Mudéjar lacework in a bell-tower so worn by time that one is tempted to stroke it.

San Juan de los Panetes is 18th-century and has a baroque-Mudéjar bell-tower, octagonal with arches and

Zaragoza, La Seo: typical Mudéjar decoration survives the Gothic intrusion.

bull's-eyes. The final double spire is Tyrolean in flavour.
San Pablo has the most beautiful tower in Zaragoza.
Happily, it does not clash with the 15th-century turrets on its
midriff. Its octagon is much richer than its counterparts in
Andalucía yet uses the familiar net pattern with restraint.
There is an arcade of blind arches and two belts of apertures
higher still are recessed. Somewhat phallic horseshoe arches
show traces of paint. Triple open arches with larger double
arches above them complete the composition. The apertures cover two-thirds of the space, which is the secret of the
serenity of the tower.
Santa María Magdalena has a tall and elaborate tower
which sparkles with diamond-shaped glazed bricks. There is
a Mudéjar apse.

Fragments of Roman wall near the **Plaza** suggest a proven-
ance for the towers of the Aljafería, while the tower of **La
Zuda** is solidified Mudéjar work on the foundations and the
footings of the Islamic citadel. Such Islamic walls as survive
have been dated to *c*.890. There are six tiers of arches over
the plain rectilinear window openings culminating in double
tiers of enriched eaves under the tile roof. The string courses
marking each tier and the massive pointed arch of the door
confirm La Zuda's relatively late date, although the building
is Almohad in its restraint. Zaragoza possesses temperate
examples of Art Nouveau, that far descendant of Mudéjar
with its neo-Islamic enthusiasm for attenuated vegetable
forms. The **General Post Office** is a turn-of-the-century
outburst of Mudéjar zest among more reticent buildings.

WALLS, TOWERS
AND SECULAR
BUILDINGS

ALBARRACÍN

OTHER SITES IN
ARAGÓN

This town endured because it was a Muslim fiefdom of El Cid.
Now it is almost buried beneath postcards and layers of
tangerine paint, to please the tourist office. It was overlooked by the rapacious government of Aragón until 1333.
Some citadel walls are 11th-century but most were rebuilt
after the Muslims departed, if they ever really did. The town
has shrunk down the hillside but some houses nestle into the
backs of towers within the inhabited area. This occupies
three sides of a triangle and stands above a high ravine
enjoying an abundance of water. Today it consists of lofty

adobe and wooden structures often projecting over or even bridging alleyways. Timber housing is exposed to the dangers of fire and rot but, most of all, neglect, of which there was plenty after the 17th-century expulsion of the Muslim craftsmen. The large street-level courting windows, not unlike grilled shops (which in one sense they were), are quaint, but antipathetic to the Muslim way of life.

ALHAMA DE ARAGÓN
The Roman spa became a Muslim one and the fine **Alcázar** was rebuilt after the conquest. The rich ochre of the local brick contrasts with the grey of other villages in this area.

AÑÓN
The village exists, in spite of its name, with a ruined castle founded by the Muslims.

ATECA
Nuestra Señora de la Paene is a converted mosque which externally retains a Moroccan form because of the height of the nave and the squat tower at the crossing which gives a hunched appearance as at Carmona and elsewhere. The Mudéjar tower is a virtuoso performance in bricks which are angled, leaning or crossed in vigorous banding.

BORJA
This in its innocence feels like a Muslim village still, although it was the stronghold of the Borgias until they left in the 14th century for Játiva en route for St Peter's and Hell.

BURBAGUENA
The Mudéjar belfry has a head-of-garlic spire in the Aragonese 'Tyrolean' manner.

CALAMOCHA
The village lies limply in the valley and possesses a small, much-repaired Islamic bridge.

CALATAYUD (*Qal 'at Ayyub* — The Castle of Job)
The **Alcázar** is square-cut on its ridge above the town and has been repaired without losing its imposing form. The fortifications date from the ninth century. Grey and sombre, the town stretches back from its railway yards; high on the

slope is the old Jewish quarter whose lanes lie in the shadows of Islamic times. The town was mostly independent and the region divided between Arab and Berber lordlings. The Mudéjar churches have fine towers.

CARIÑENA
The town became a knightly fief. All that remains of its Islamic past is a bell-tower. Towers of a cement factory make good substitutes for an *Alcázar*. The church of **Santiago** dominates the town and was converted out of a mosque.

DAROCA
Charles V rebuilt the walls and achieved 114 towers, planting them as other mere mortals plant trees. **San Domingo de Silos** has a fine stone apse and the **Colegiata de Santa María** also has Mudéjar towers, but that of **San Miguel** is finer.

HUESCA
A line of walls and Islamic street contours survive. Parts of the walls and floor of an early solid tower have been excavated. The cathedral, *c*.1500, has a Mudéjar gallery built of brick, and one arch of the Friday Mosque survives.

LONGARES
The 14th-century Mudéjar tower is crowned with a turret choked by a ruff, making it look like a minaret.

MALUENDA
This is one of several local towns and villages with rewarding Mudéjar churches.

PANIZA
Still the guardian of the pass, the village has a Mudéjar belfry for its watch-tower.

RUEDA DE JALÓN
The Islamic stronghold belongs to the ninth century, if not before. A fortress on a crag, it is as haggard as a toothless crone, for the rock is riddled with caves.

SAN MARTÍN DEL RÍO
The church has an unusual hexagonal Mudéjar tower.

TARAZONA

This is a Mudéjar town. The **cathedral** is on the site of a Mozarab church and details pay homage to La Seo of Zaragoza. The brick tower is restrained but the cloisters are Mudéjar, with spirited leaping arches. **La Magdalena** has a high bell-tower and the quality of the brickwork is noteworthy, as is the tower of nearby **San Miguel**.

TAUSTE

The 13th-century Mudéjar tower of **Santa María** is exceptionally lofty and richly adorned in a style typical of Aragón.

TERUEL

Teruel: Plaza Carlos Castel with the Art Nouveau bank (left).

The city was a centre of Islamic power until as late in the process of reconquest as 1171, when it surrendered and the large Muslim population was permitted to stay. It was the Jews who were attacked and expelled in 1586, while the Muslims remained until the disastrous expulsions at the beginning of the 17th century. Every man and woman left to enrich North Africa with their skills, leaving Aragón without masons, carpenters, saddlers, cordwainers, weavers or farriers and all those trades which make civilization possible. Frantic appeals were made to Castile for craftsmen to fill the empty workshops and homes. The town suffered terribly during the Civil War but has now spread across all the encircling heights so that old Teruel is a place apart. A strangely shaped plaza drifts downwards past an Art Nouveau bank and the smallest public monument (a miniature bull) in Spain. It also has an example of the late Mudéjar revival style in the shady grand staircase leading down to the station, flanked by a fantastic collection of lamps.

The church of **San Pedro** dates from the 13th to 14th centuries and was rebuilt in the 18th. Its tower is the simplest of the four great Mudéjar monuments but is surely the finest example of Mudéjar decoration. Standing on large, once Roman, stone footings, it spans a passage above a sharply pointed arch. The brick designs are studded with green or blue glazed diamonds and the colonnettes are glazed too, becoming brown at the top. The lower section has an arch with a course of blue columns above and a blind colonnade protected by a projecting brick string course. The second level has three pairs of deep windows, recessed three times with three pairs of green columns each. Above is a blind run of green columns with triangular brick piers between and over this are rows of diamonds and double windows with free-standing columns dividing them, their capitals foliate. Green-glazed and plain bricks alternate in voussoirs. Yet a new pattern of columns and circles follows, with a run of blue and green diamonds alternating above. There is a mid-section of brown colonnettes with circles above and below and the pattern is then repeated in reverse. The whole composition is repeated on three sides but on the fourth nothing can be seen, although the tower is detached from the church. To pass under the arch is to appreciate the thickness of the tower. The apsidal end of the church is decorated with familiar Mudéjar strapwork nets punctuated by star-shaped tiles and crested by little turrets.

Sentimental rather than aesthetic, the tomb of the 13th-century 'Amantes de Teruel' is set in a chapel devoted to this Romeo and Juliet whose love was forbidden by their families. Their alabaster figures were executed in Mudéjar style by Juan de Ávalos in the 20th century.

The cathedral of **Santa María** was often altered until the 17th century. Its tower is an elaborate version of that of San Pedro, with the top arcade ornate with white columns and paired windows below a bell-turret capped with a lantern. There is strapwork in the buttresses of the main dome and remains of it in the apse. The portal is a hideous pastiche of the Mudéjar style, resulting from an attempt to recapture the past without understanding it. The brown mosaic rings of San Pedro have become the flat bottoms of jeroboams. Inside, facilely faked stonework neatly ruled is monumentally dreary. The ceiling, however, is painted sumptuously with scenes of craftsmen that survive spotlighting. The star created by leaping arches in the dome pays the usual homage to La Mezquita.

The **Torre de San Martín** is early 14th-century, restored in the 16th and 20th, and embodies all that Mudéjar could achieve. *Azulejos* and details abound and the green colonnettes of San Pedro are now twins between white balls. Only the bell cage is sober. Although such square towers spring from the Almoravid and Almohad tradition, of which La Giralda in Sevilla is the finest example in Spain, nothing remains here of the purity of La Giralda except the proportions, masked by dazzling surfaces.

Teruel: the ideal Mudéjar tower of San Pedro.

Teruel: the tower of San Martín.

Teruel: the star-spangled tower of San Salvador.

The tower of **San Salvador** acts as a gate to the town and excels San Martín in the quality of its tiles. It gains because such towers are more dramatic when set in narrow streets and not, like San Martín, standing totally exposed.

TOBED
An Arabic inscription in the parish church professes the Faith and could not be more Mudéjar, entwined with an elaborate decorative entanglement fit for the Sleeping Beauty.

TORRIGO
The Mudéjar tower is elaborate and tall enough to have four tiers ending in a modest, tiled cap.

UTEBO
Santa María is a Mudéjar church built early in the 16th century by Antonio de Sariñena; the brick tower by Alonso de Loznes is built in two halves. The bottom is rectangular like La Zuda, Zaragoza: the upper, an elaborated octagon, is out of key. *Azulejos* highlight the composition.

Some northern provinces possess a few Visigothic and Mozarabic monuments and towns with traces of Islamic rule.

OTHER PROVINCES

ASTURIAS
Oviedo: church of San Miguel de Linio/Lillo, dated 848; Muslim window.

CANTABRIA
La Hermida: 8km (5 miles) away is the fine Visigothic church of Santa María de Lebeña (839).

CATALUNYA/CANTALUÑA
Balaguer: Islamic walls.
Girona/Gerona: Mudéjar *hammam*. Near Ullastret is Mozarabic San Julián de Buada.
LLeida/Lérida: traces of the Islamic town.
LLançá: Mozarabic monastery of Sant Pere/San Pedro de Roda.
Terrassa: San Miguel, San Pedro and Santa María de Marquet.
Tortosa: traces of the Muslim period.

GALICIA
Bande: Visigothic Santa Comba.
Celanova, near Ourense/Orense: Mozarabic chapel of San Miguel.

NAVARRA
Tudela: Muslim work in Santa María la Mayor.

RIOJA
San Millán de la Cogolla: Mozarabic church of San Millán de Susa, founded as a hermitage in 537, consecrated in 929 and burnt by al-Mansur in 1102. Its portable altar is now in the Archaeological Museum in Madrid.

GLOSSARY

Ajaracas   trelliswork brick design often decorating Mudéjar apses

Ajimez   small pairs of windows divided by a column or pier

Albarrani   a projected tower joined to the main wall by a bridge

Alcazaba   Islamic fortress, usually on a height

Alcázar   Islamic fortified palace

Arrabal   city quarter or district

Artesonado   elaborate wooden coffered ceiling

Ayuntamiento   town hall

Azulejo   glazed tiles frequently forming star patterns common to Spain and North Africa, especially Morocco

Coro   a walled choir usually found in the centre of a church

Granja   farmstead

Hammam   public hot bathing rooms based on the Roman system

Iglesia   church

Judería   Jewish quarter

Khan   an inn for merchants with cells for storage below and for rest above

Kufic/Qufic   a very early formalized Arabic script

Madrasa   college for students of law and religion, inseparable in Islam

Mampostería   a rough concrete made of rubble

Maqsura   an elevated platform, usually with grilles

Mezquita   a mosque but especially La Mezquita of Córdoba

Mihrab   a recess, alcove, arch or any indication of the direction of Mecca

Mirador   belvedere

Morisco   baptized Muslim

Mozarab   Christians living under Islamic rule and the name given to churches, etc, built by them

Mudéjar   Muslims working for Christian masters; the name given to their architectural style

Muqarnas   the hanging masonry effect resulting from the multiple use of support elements

Seo   cathedral

Tapia   a type of mud brick

English Architectural Terms

Ashlar   carefully cut stone

Console   decorative masonry support for a balcony, etc

Imposts   the usually projecting stone from which an arch springs

Interlace   decoration which crosses under and over corresponding elements

Machicoulis   hole in ceiling of a large gateway through which missiles, etc, could be dropped

Merlon   the section of a battlement, etc, each side of the embrasures

Mole   a massive wall projecting as a breakwater, etc

Narthex   the forehall of a church

Spoglia   materials re-used from buildings in ruins

Squinch   corner support to a dome made up of sections

Voussoir   the wedge-shaped stones which create the form of an arch or vault

SELECT BIBLIOGRAPHY

Past work on the art of Islamic Spain is marked by a number of notable books. More recently, a very considerable number of studies have been published mainly in journals and occasional papers of which only a selection can be presented here.

Bargebuhr, F.P., *The Alhambra: A Cycle of Studies on the 11th century in Moorish Spain*, Berlin, 1965

Dickie, J., (Yakub Zeki), 'The Alhambra: some reflections prompted ...' in *Studia Arabica et Islamica*, Beirut, 1981

Esco, C., Giraut, J., Senac, P., *Arqueología Islámica de la Marca Superior de al-Andalus*, Huesca, 1988

Ewert, C., 'Tipología de la mezquita en Occidente de los Amayas a los Almohades', *Congreso de Arqueología Medieval Española*, Vol 1, pp. 180–204, Madrid, 1987

Fernández-Puertas, A., (from a vast range of works on the Islamic palaces and the Alhambra, in particular) *Prologue* to F. Hernández Giménez, *Madinat al-Zahra'*, Granada, 1955

Glick, T.F., *Islamic and Christian Spain in the Early Middle Ages*, Princeton, 1979

Gómez Moreno, M., 'Arte arabe basta los Almohodes; Arte Mozarabe' in *Ars Hispaniae*, Vol 4, Madrid, 1949

Lévi-Provençal, E., *Histoire de l'Espagne musulmane*, 3 vols, Paris-Leiden, 1950-59

Sánchez Albornoz, C., *La España musulmana*, 2 vols, Buenos Aires, 1946

Torres Balbas, L., 'Arte Almohade, arte Nazarí, arte Mudéjar' in *Ars Hispaniae*, Vol 4, Madrid, 1949

Torres Balbas, L., and Terrasse, H., *Ciudades hispano-musulmanas*, 2 vols, Madrid, 1972

Wasserstein, D., *The Rise and Fall of the Party Kings; Politics and Society in Islamic Spain 1002–1086*, Princeton, 1985

Zozaya, J., 'Islamic fortifications in Spain; some aspects', in *Papers in Iberian Archaeology, B.A.R. 193*, Oxford, 1984

Important works by Professor Bosworth and others are not listed because these are not exclusively concerned with Islamic Spain.

There are many peripheral books, among which are the works of W. Montgomery Watt, including *Islamic Survey* No. 9: 'The Influence of Islam on Medieval Europe' and the always stimulating two volumes of Bernard Lewis, *Islam*, Harper, Torchbooks, 1974. There is also comedy to be found in Helen Waddell's masterpiece, *The Wandering Scholars*, Constable, 1926, in a style as civilized as it is out of fashion.

TABLE OF RULERS OF SPAIN IN THE MUSLIM PERIOD

UMAYYADS
'Abd ar-Rahman I, 756–788
Hisham I, 788–796
al-Hakam I, 796–822
'Abd ar-Rahman II, 822–852
Muhammad I, 852–886
al-Mundhir, 886-888
'Abd-Allah, 888–912
'Abd ar-Rahman III, Caliph, 912–961
al-Hakam II, Caliph, 961–976
Hisham II, Caliph, 976–1009; 1010–1013
al-Mansur (Almanzor), Vezir, 976–1002
Muhammad II, 1009 and 1010; Sulaiman 1009
    and 1013; 'Abd ar-Rahman V, 1023;
Muhammad III, 1024-7; Hisham III, 1027-31

Alfonso I of the Asturias, 739–757
Alfonso II, 792–842

Ordoño I, 850–866
Alfonso III, 866–910

Ordoño II, King of León, 910–925
Ramiro II of León, 931–950
Ramiro III of León, 966–982
Alfonso V, 999–1028

MULUK at-TAWAIF — REYES DE TAIFAS
Hammudids of Malaga and Algeciras, 1010-
1057
Abbadids of Sevilla, 1023–1091
Jahwarids of Córdoba, 1031–1069
Aftasids of Badajoz, 1022–1094
Dhu'n-Nunids of Toledo, before 1028–1085
'Amirids of Valencia, 1021–1096
Tujibids and Hudids of Zaragoza, 1019–1142

Fernando I of Castile and León, 1035–1065

Ramiro I of Aragón, 1035–1063
Alfonso VI of Castile and León 1065–1109
Sancho I of Aragón, 1063–1094

ALMORAVIDS
Yusuf ibn-Tashfin, 1061–1106
'Ali, 1106–1142
Tashfin, 1142–1146
Ibrahim, 1146
Ishaq, 1146–1147

Alfonso I of Aragón, 1104–1134
Alfonso VII of Castile and León, 1126–1157
Petronila of Aragón, 1137–1162
Sancho III of Castile, 1157–1158
Fernando II of León, 1157–1188

ALMOHADS
Abu Yaqub Yusuf, 1163–1184
Abu Yusuf Ya'qub al-Mansur, 1184–1199

Muhammad an-Nasir, 1199–1214

Abu Ya'qub Yusuf II al-Mustansir, 1214
(Almohad withdrawal from Spain)

Alfonso II of Aragón, 1162–1196
Alfonso VIII of Castile, 1158–1214
Alfonso IX of León, 1188–1229
Pedro II of Aragón, 1196–1213
Fernando III of Castille and Leon, 1217–1252
Jaime I of Aragón, 1213–1276
Alfonso X of Castile and León, 1252–1284
Pedro III of Aragoń, 1276–1285

NASRIDS OF GRANADA
Muhammad I, 1232-1272
Muhammad II, 1272-1302
Muhammad III, 1302-1308
Nasr, 1308-1313
Isma'il I, 1313-1325
Muhammad IV, 1325-1333
Yusuf I, 1333-1354

Muhammad V, 1354-1359 and 1362-1391
Ismail II, 1359-1360
Muhammad VI, 1360-1362

Yusuf II, 1391-1395
Muhammad VII, 1395-1407
Yusuf III, 1407-1417
Muhammad VIII, 1417-1419, 1427-1430
Muhammad IX, 1419-1427, 1430-1432,
 1432-1445
Yusuf IV, 1432
Muhammad X, 1445, 1446-1447
Yusuf V, 1445-1446, 1462
Sa'd al-Musta'ın, 1453-1462, 1462-1464

'Ali, 1464-1482, 1483
Muhammad XI (Boabdil), 1482-1483,
 1487-1492
Muhammad XII, 1485-1486

Sancho IV of Castile and León, 1284-1295
Jaime II of Aragón, 1291-1327
Fernando IV of Castile and León, 1295-1312
Alfonso XI of Castile and León, 1312-1350
Alfonso IV of Aragón, 1327-1336
Pedro IV of Aragón, 1336-1387
Pedro I of Castile and León, the Cruel,
 1350-1367, 1367-1369
Enrique II Trastamara of Castile and León
 1366-1367, 1369-1379

Various Kings of Castile and Aragón,
 1387-1474

{ Isabella of Castile and León, 1474-1504
 Fernando II of Castile and V of Aragón,
  1479-1516
 Charles V, 1516-1556

MUSEUMS

This cannot be a list of all the museums of Spain, let alone the world, which have Islamic, Visigoth, Jewish or Mozarabic treasures. Each provincial capital has its museum even though many have had the cream of their possessions carried off to Madrid. Other towns, too, have exhibits worth noting, such as Lugo in Galicia, with interesting local material in the pleasant Diputación. Of foreign museums, in France the Musée Historique des Tissus, Lyon, should be visited. In Madrid are the Museo Arqueológico, the most outstanding museum in Spain, and when it reopens (which will only be on one or two days a week) the Instituto de Valencia de Don Juan; the Instituto Lázaro Galdiano is of interest for its Granada silks in particular. The Museo del Armería Real at the Palacio Real and the Manuscript Library in the Escorial (open only by special permission), are of interest.

List of provincial museums

Barcelona:	Museo de la Academia de las Ciencias
	Museo Arqueológico
Burgos:	Monasterio de las Huelgas: Museo de Ricas Telas
Córdoba:	Museo Arqueológico
	Museo de la Torre Calahorra
	Museo de la Excavación de Madinat az-Zahra'
Girona:	Cathedral sacristy
Granada:	Museo Nacional de Arte Hispano-Musulman
León:	Museo Arqueológico
Malaga:	Museo Arqueológico
Oviedo:	Cathedral museum, tragically damaged in 1977; exhibits under repair
Pamplona:	Cathedral refectory
Sevilla:	Museo Arqueológico
Toledo:	Cathedral: Ropería
	Taller del Moro
	San Román
Valladolid:	Museo Arqueológico
Zamora:	Museo Arqueológico
Zaragoza:	Museo Arqueológico

ACKNOWLEDGEMENTS

Photographs
The publishers would particularly like to thank C. M. Dixon for his help with the photography for this book. The author: p. 92; Douglas Dickins: pp. 11, 22, 38, 64, 88; C. M. Dixon: jacket photograph and pp. 7, 14, 15, 17 (bottom), 23, 25, 27, 28, 29, 31, 34, 36, 37, 54, 55, 56, 59, 60, 61, 62, 69, 71, 75, 76, 77, 78 (top), 81, 85, 91, 97, 98, 99, 100, 102, 108, 109, 110, 113, 120, 125, 126, 128, 132, 133, 134, 138, 139, 140; A. F. Kersting: pp. vi, 18, 30, 46, 48, 51, 73, 104, 122; Museo Arqueológico Nacional, Madrid: p. 10; Museum of the History of Science, Oxford: p. 12; Patrimonio Nacional, Madrid: p. 3; Ronald Sheridan/Ancient Art and Architecture Collection: pp. 17 (top), 52, 74, 111, 114; Peter Townsend: pp. 72, 78 (bottom).

Author's Acknowledgements
The author has received innumerable kindnesses from a great number of people in Spain and in particular from Dr Juan Zozaya. In London, he has been able to seek advice from Professor Don Antonio Fernández-Puertas and encouragement from David Catillejo, as well as from Miss Venetia Porter of the British Museum. Dr James Dickie (Yakub Zéki) patiently read the text and purified the transliterative system with remarkable good humour. My errors are my own and certainly not those of my editor, Gabrielle Townsend, who laboured hard and long to make this book presentable. I am most grateful to her.

My wife and son have driven or travelled with me with remarkable fortitude, and their critical observations have been invaluable.

INDEX

INDEX